Extra͏ Mon͏

in an Ordinary Life

Mike Preston

O&U
Onwards & Upwards

Onwards and Upwards Publishers

4 The Old Smithy, London Road,
Rockbeare, EX5 2EA,
United Kingdom

www.onwardsandupwards.org

First edition, published in the United Kingdom by Onwards and Upwards Publishers Ltd. (2022).

ISBN: 978-1-78815-975-3
Typeface: Sabon LT

Even when I am old and grey, do not forsake me, my God, till I declare your power to the next generation, your mighty acts to all who are to come.

Psalm 71:18

Extraordinary Moments

Contents

Extraordinary Moments

About the Author

Mike Preston was working in offshore banking and finance, when, at the age of thirty, he was diagnosed with myalgic encephalomyelitis. After his miraculous healing, he became actively involved in local church ministry and eventually was ordained as an Elim minister. Mike has pastored churches in Guernsey, England and Scotland and is married and has three children and three grandchildren.

To contact the author, please write to:

Mike Preston
c/o Onwards and Upwards Publishers
4 The Old Smithy, London Road, Exeter, EX5 2EA

Or send an email to:

mikepreston1961@hotmail.co.uk

Extraordinary Moments

Foreword by John Glass

I have known the author of this book for several years. I am always impressed by those who, having proven themselves and excelled in a professional capacity, take up a call to serve in Christian ministry. There are many similarities between secular and spiritual leadership, but several differences too. It is not always easy for those who have held managerial roles in industry to sit in the 'second chair' as part of someone else's team and support another person's vision. The reason why Mike Preston was able to do this, I quickly observed, was because of his gracious nature and servant heart. It has been rightly said that "those who are too big to serve are also too small to lead". It was inevitable, therefore, that at some juncture Mike would assume the role of senior leader in a church of his own.

In the pages that follow you will find yourself engaging with a narrative of God's supernatural intervention that spans not only decades but continents, and that reveals a God who concerns Himself not only with large and seminal moments of our destiny but also in the more minor details of our daily life.

Too often narratives of this nature seem only to seek to amplify the author's achievements, but you will not find that attitude here. Written with humility and vulnerability, what follows offers is a lens through which the Lord is magnified, and which subsequently encourages us to extend our faith to believe that even when we feel that destiny has led us into a *cul-*

de-sac and we can see no visible way forward, God is able to make a way.

One of the most compelling descriptions of spirituality that I find in the Old Testament is in the first Psalm, where we are offered the analogy of a fruitful tree planted by rivers of water. The word 'planted' is especially important. It implies intentional placement rather than the random sowing of a seed. Many characters throughout Scripture find themselves in 'less than comfortable' situations and struggle with the environment in which they have been planted. Yet when they realise they have been positioned there for a purpose, God's plan becomes clearer. As you read, and I trust are encouraged by the accounts that follow through this book, you will find several similar parallels.

John Glass

General Superintendent Elim Churches 2000-2016
Chair of Council, Evangelical Alliance 2014-2018

Introduction

I was contemplating calling this book 'Walking in the Supernatural with God', which would sound like a great title for a book about the life of Kathryn Kuhlman or Smith Wigglesworth or another of 'God's Generals' – men and women whose exceptional ministries have been etched into modern church history and impacted and inspired thousands of believers. However, it is not about such stalwarts of faith; it's about my ordinary life in which I have experienced an extraordinary Holy Spirit, and therefore *Extraordinary Moments in an Ordinary Life* seemed more appropriate.

The purpose of this book is simply to give glory and thanks to a wonderful God who has deemed that my humble and unassuming existence is worth enriching with his glorious presence.

I often personalise Psalm 8:4 and ask God, "What am I that you are mindful of me, and the son of man that you care for me?"

And yet God has been so real to me, and the evidence for his power and intervention in my life and in the lives of close friends of mine will be told in the pages that follow. I hope and pray that you will be inspired and encouraged by a story of an ordinary man who will never be known beyond his family and circle of friends but who, from time to time, walked in the supernatural with God. This was made possible only through the Holy Spirit.

Extraordinary Moments

1

An Outpouring of the Holy Spirit in Blantyre, Malawi

David carefully negotiated the potholes in the dusty road leading up the hill to the Chilobwe Church of God in Blantyre. It was Sunday, 6th March 2005, the sun was already hot and each jolt of the Land Rover was jarring. It was as if we were on some immensely uncomfortable and torturous funfair ride. We had just passed the house of the local witchdoctor who practised his occultic arts there at the foot of the hill. There are many witchdoctors in Malawi, and their influence permeates throughout the whole of the nation's society and government.

As we arrived at the church carpark on the summit of the hill, we could hear the congregation singing. David Le Page, my missionary friend and mentor, had collected the Land Rover at Lilongwe airport from Pastor Lizimba, the Church of God National Leader, and we had driven down to Blantyre the day before, visiting the wonderful Dedza Pottery en route.

I felt nervous about preaching at the Church of God National Pastors' Conference because I had never preached through an interpreter before. I went to bed praying for God to help me and give me courage, wisdom, power and peace – and I woke the next morning speaking in tongues[1]! I felt equipped, empowered and ready. As David parked the Land Rover, one man ran out to meet us and insisted on carrying my briefcase and my bible into the church for me. The brick-built church building was packed to the doors with over 250 people attending the first morning of the National Pastors' Conference, and I was the guest speaker. As I made my way down the aisle to the platform, I noticed that everyone in the congregation was sitting on wooden backless benches and the national leadership team were all sitting on white plastic patio chairs on the platform. I was invited to sit on one of these chairs.

The wonderful African singing finished and Pastor Lizimba introduced David Le Page, who was well known to all of the pastors as he had spent over thirty years living in Malawi preaching the gospel and planting churches, helping build them with the local labourers. He was usually instrumental in getting the hardwood trusses and the corrugated iron roofs, often paid for by missions donations. His principle was that the earnest desire of the people should be demonstrated through their collaboration locally in organizing the brick-making and building work. He would commonly supervise the design and the foundations, and then wait until the building was at roof height before then helping with the roof.

David, in turn, introduced me as the speaker that morning, and I stood to face the congregation. I felt the power of the Holy Spirit come upon me, and I began to speak about the Holy Spirit and how Jesus cried out to the crowd in Jerusalem saying:

---

[1] Speaking in tongues is where a person speaks or prays in an unlearned language given to them by the Holy Spirit.

'Let anyone who is thirsty come to me and drink.
Whoever believes in me, as Scripture has said, rivers
of living water will flow from within them.' By this
he meant the Spirit, whom those who believed in him
were later to receive.

John 7:37-39

I walked up and down the platform enacting the collecting of the water from the Pool of Siloam by the priests, and carrying it up to the temple where it would be poured out on the altar as a libation offering, and how that symbolised the coming of the Holy Spirit being poured out. My interpreter followed me and copied my actions, pretending to carry a vessel of water on his shoulders too. I preached for an hour and a half, and then I asked Pastor Lizimba if I could pray for the pastors to receive the Holy Spirit.

I had been preparing my talks for the conference whilst on a plane flying from London to Mexico on a business trip just three months earlier, and I had felt the Holy Spirit impress upon me to both preach on the Holy Spirit and to pray for the pastors. I thought that it was an odd thing that the Holy Spirit had asked, as the Church of God was a Pentecostal organisation and I imagined that most, if not all, of the pastors would be baptised in the Holy Spirit. When I mentioned it to David, he said that I should do it and see what happened. So David, Pastor Lizimba and I started to move along the rows of pastors sitting on benches, and I placed my hands on the heads of two pastors at a time and prayed simply, "Holy Spirit, come." *He came.*

I have never heard such a sound before: the roar of voices as the room full of pastors spoke out in tongues, one by one receiving the baptism in the Holy Spirit. As we prayed for the

3

pastors, I looked across at Pastor Lizimba and he had tears streaming down his face as he prayed for these men. It was a tremendous, powerful and yet heart-melting moment. The noise of tongues reached a crescendo and continued for ten minutes or more, and then suddenly in complete unison it stopped. I made my way back to my white plastic patio chair on the platform, and Pastor Lizimba went up to the microphone and asked in the main Malawi language of Chichewa how many pastors had received the baptism in the Holy Spirit and spoken in tongues for the first time. Over fifty pastors put their hands up.

This was truly an extraordinary moment in my ordinary life, one of the milestones in my journey of faith. There were many potholes on my spiritual road, and I did not negotiate them all successfully. Yet God, in his sovereign power and in accordance with his plan for my life, had brought me safely to this point when I would once more humbly thank him for his grace and his goodness in my life. When I look back, I see his hand of mercy on me, so let me share with you some of this journey right now.

2

Back to the Beginning

My own Holy Spirit story has its roots in an event which occurred in 1911. The Batiste family made their way to the Cobo Mission Hall, in Guernsey in the Channel Islands, to hear special speaker Rev. Robert Davies, who had come from the Welsh revival. Guernsey is an island of twenty-four square miles, lying in the Bay of St Malo, just ninety miles south of the English Coast. This is an island which was visited by John Wesley in 1787 and Charles Spurgeon in 1889.

The preaching on the Holy Spirit was rejected by a number of people that morning, so he was unable to continue. However, a few people were curious and they all met with the speaker at the home of Mr Batiste, who lived just inland from Vazon Bay. It was Saturday, 19th August 1911, and as they listened to the preacher, the power of God fell on them like on the Day of Pentecost and they were all filled with the Holy Spirit and spoke in tongues. Mr Batiste was a tomato-grower with a packing shed where he would pack his tomatoes for export, and so, with help from others, he made seats from wooden planks lying astride tomato boxes, and the inaugural meeting of the Vazon Mission took place, with a horse tethered in the corner of his packing shed!

I am not sure exactly when my grandmother Druscilla Ferbrache started to attend the Vazon Mission, whether it was as a young woman or after she married my grandfather William Frederick Guille during the First World War – but she did, and so did my mother Irene Guille after she was born in 1925, along with her five siblings.

People from the area used to come and peer through the windows of the mission hall during the services to see these people who were rumoured to be "climbing the walls" under the influence of the Holy Spirit.

In 1920 George Jeffreys visited Guernsey and conducted some evangelistic meetings. As a result, 'The Vazon Mission' decided then to join the Elim Movement and become an Elim Alliance Church. A large crusade was held in February 1926 led by Rev. George Jeffreys, and up to nine hundred people attended the meetings in St George's Hall in St Peter Port, Guernsey. Two more Elim churches were established in the Island in 1934 and 1936.

In June 1940 my grandmother and her children were evacuated from the Island due to the impending invasion by the German military forces, and sailed to Weymouth where they were put on a train to Bury in Lancashire and given a council home to live in. My grandfather stayed behind to organise for someone to live in the family home and then, on 28th June, he too headed for the harbour. That day, the Luftwaffe arrived and six Heinkel He 111 bombers destroyed a line of lorries on the quay loaded with tomatoes for export, and thirty-four people died. That night, the SS Isle of Sark, a cross-channel ferry, sailed for England with 647 refugees, including my grandfather, and it was the last ship to sail from the Island until the end of the war.

My family in Bury looked for an Elim Church to attend that first Sunday after their arrival, but could only find an Assemblies of God church – a sister church to Elim, founded by Stephen Jeffreys. They walked in that Sunday morning and were greeted by the elders and seated; then my mother noticed a young man taking the offering and her sister noticed his best friend. It was not long before that young man, Vernon Preston, was courting my mother, and her sister Daphne was courting his best friend Bert Howcroft.

My mother and father married in Bury on 21st July 1945.

During this time in Bury, they both attended a Smith Wigglesworth evangelism and healing meeting in Preston, and after the meeting, where many people were healed, an invitation was given to go into a side room if anyone wanted to be baptised in the Holy Spirit. They went in and sat together and both received the baptism of the Holy Spirit and spoke in tongues.

In 1946, when it was safe to return to Guernsey, the family moved back to the Island and continued to attend the Vazon Elim Mission Hall.

I was born in 1961 into a churchgoing family with parents who often prayed in tongues, and both my mother and father would from time to time give messages in tongues in a service.

I was taught about the Holy Spirit and I witnessed many healings, miracles and, on one occasion, was told to "play in the garden" whilst a young man was delivered from demon possession in our front room by the pastor and my parents.

I attended the Vazon Mission Hall every Sunday morning and evening, and it was always packed with people, usually around a hundred men, women and children, and I enjoyed the singing and the Sunday school. One Sunday morning in 1969, at the age of eight, I was listening to the gospel being preached by a missionary, David Le Page, who was back in the Island on furlough, that same missionary whom I accompanied to Malawi in 2005, thirty-six years later. I became so convicted and convinced that I needed Jesus as my Saviour that I asked my mother if I could leave the meeting and go and sit in the car outside as I did not feel very well. As I sat there in the back seat of my father's red Austin 1100, I could hear the final hymn being sung – "Pass me not, O gentle Saviour, do not pass me by, while on others thou art calling, do not pass me by." Tears were flowing down my cheeks as I sat there and then prayed a simple prayer, inviting Jesus into my heart.

My journey of faith began that very day.

Before I go any further, I must point out that I was an extremely shy boy and all my school reports during my early years mention this. I had no great aspirations, I considered myself to be unimportant and never imagined that one day I would experience powerful encounters with the Holy Spirit which I will be telling of in this book.

When I was fourteen years old, I changed almost overnight from a nervous and shy recluse to a young man who, inspired by Christian singer and songwriter Larry Norman, asked for a guitar for Christmas and then proceeded to teach myself guitar by playing Larry Norman songs.

In 1976, when I was fifteen, a group of three girls and three boys from church decided to go to an Elim Camp in the Isle of Wight where singer-songwriter Len Magee was helping out. We had an amazing time each evening in the main tent, with great worship and teaching, and one night many of the young people there received the baptism in the Holy Spirit and spoke in tongues. When I got home again, my mother said that she had been praying that I too would have been baptised in the Holy Spirit. Somehow, though, it just did not happen for me. Even in our youth group we had a 'waiting meeting' and my brother David, who was the youth leader, prayed for me to receive the baptism in the Holy Spirit, but nothing happened. My encounter with the Holy Spirit was yet to come.

There were great opportunities for anyone who could sing or play an instrument to take part in the coffee bars which were held regularly at church. It was not long before I formed a band with two good friends, Carl and Nigel, and in 1977 I began an adventure in music and gospel outreach, for the next ten years writing songs and performing in bands in churches, youth clubs and even a local hotel, sharing the gospel wherever I went.

I had been the only Christian in my year at the Guernsey Grammar School For Boys, and was bullied for it on a regular basis, often coming home with my school blazer covered in spit as the boys in my year had mocked me for my faith. I refused to deny my faith, and God was faithful to me: in the third year, two boys, Steve and Mark, started the September term by telling everyone they had been on a Pathfinder camp over the summer holidays and had both given their lives to Jesus. Suddenly I had backup. Steve became my best friend and he was my best man at my wedding in 1981.

The interest in Christianity grew within the school, especially when a Christian Union was established, and I had the joy of seeing many of my school friends become Christians before they left the sixth form.

I joined the merchant bank Kleinwort Benson straight from school in 1979 and began a career in banking and finance, which took my focus off church. Wanting to follow in the footsteps of my older brother Phil, I was determined to be as successful as he had been in banking, having been appointed as a bank CEO in his late twenties.

It just did not happen for me. I jumped from bank to bank trying to advance my career, but I was overlooked for promotion time and time again. I even left the finance industry and became the Financial Director of a publishing company to try and find success, but when the economic bubble burst in 1989 and the publishing company went into receivership, I went back into finance and still struggled to move into management. All thoughts about serving God and seeking the baptism in the Holy Spirit were far from my mind.

In January 1991, I fell ill. I will recount exactly what happened in the next chapter, however, it was a turning point in my walk with God. In 1993, aged thirty-two, I was driving along the coast road past Cobo Bay on my way home from a prayer meeting, singing a song that we had sung in worship, and I suddenly realised that I was singing in a language I had not learnt; I had received the baptism in the Holy Spirit, and from that moment everything changed. My ordinary life was thereafter invaded by extraordinary moments and miracles. Often people have asked me why I believe what I believe, and I think that reading this book might explain why I have never doubted the existence of a loving God and the truth of his Word.

3

Miracles

Living in this postmodern and secular society, the subject of miracles is rarely discussed and freely dismissed as fanciful and tripe. The dictionary definition of a miracle is:

> *An extraordinary and welcome event that is not explicable by natural or scientific laws and is therefore attributed to a divine agency.*[2]

There are numerous examples of miracles in the life of Jesus and in accounts of the early church. Miracles have always featured in church history in the lives and ministries of men and women of faith.

I have no problems with miracles. Think about it. Every living cell is programmed. If it is programmed then there must be a programmer. You could not justifiably claim that the Microsoft Word programme that I am using to type this book happened by random selection or from an explosion out of nothing. So if God is the eternal Spirit who programmed everything in life, including the fine balance of nature, then just

---

[2] Definition from Google; powered by Oxford Languages.

as a software designer can at any time they desire overwrite their programme, likewise God can overwrite the programme in any living cell and any aspect of nature. We call these moments miracles.

In my ordinary life I have experienced extraordinary moments and happenings that cannot be explained by natural or scientific laws, and I would like to share some of these with you.

Healed of Pernicious Anaemia

Until the 1920s, people who were diagnosed with pernicious anaemia died, often after many years of suffering. The first treatments used liver therapy. Patients were fed raw, or very lightly cooked, liver several times a day. The liver could be fried, grilled or made into liver drinks. Later, liver injections became available, and in the late 1940s, artificially produced B12 became available.

Pernicious anaemia is defined as a type of vitamin B12 deficiency that results from impaired uptake of vitamin B12 due to the lack of a substance known as intrinsic factor (IF) produced by the stomach lining. Vitamin B12 helps the body make healthy red blood cells and helps keep nerve cells healthy. It is found in animal foods, including meat, fish, eggs, milk and other dairy products.

The most common cause of pernicious anaemia is the loss of stomach cells that make intrinsic factor. Intrinsic factor helps the body absorb vitamin B12 in the intestine. Although pernicious anaemia can be easily treated by regular injections of B12, there is no known cure to reverse the condition and for the body to once again naturally produce B12.

My mother told her story in our church newsletter in 2002, so rather than rewrite it, here is her story in her own words:

It is now seventeen years since I received a healing touch from the Lord. He has healed me many times but this was a *miracle* of healing. Sometime in 1975-1976, I can't remember the exact date, I began to feel very, very tired, not occasionally but all the time. I have always been very active and wanting to be doing things, besides looking after my home and my family; suddenly I felt very fatigued and often fell asleep on the settee. This is so unusual (even today at seventy-seven years of age). I remember we were going on holiday, so I thought that this would be what would put me right. Just before going away, I did visit my doctor and told him how I felt, so he did lots of blood tests, which he forwarded to the hospital for further testing. When we returned from holiday, I felt rested and refreshed for a short while and then all the weariness returned worse than ever; so back I went to the doctor. "I'm sorry, Mrs Preston," he said, "but I have some bad news for you. The results of the tests we did about three weeks ago tell us that you have pernicious anaemia." I had heard of this complaint and knew that it could be serious. He then said that I had to go to the hospital and have injections of B12 as this was seriously lacking in my blood. So, I duly went and had an injection. The doctor had informed me that the condition was incurable and also I would need injections for the rest of my life. I started with monthly injections and confess that after having them I felt decidedly better. After some time, I had to have them every three weeks. I knew when I needed an injection as I felt washed out and extremely weary. This continued for several years and then we had a special Jamaican evangelist called George Millar who came to the Island and took a series of services at the Beau Sejour Theatre. My husband and I have been Christians since we were quite young and went to our Pentecostal church regularly. We believed that Jesus Christ who had become our saviour was also able to heal the sick. Many times I had experienced healing for minor things in my life, but on 5th November 1983, I received my miracle of healing.

We had sung, and prayer had been made; a soloist had sung some beautiful songs about Jesus. Our own minister, Pastor Marriott, had read a Bible reading from Mark's Gospel chapter 10, verses 46 to 52. This part of the Scripture recorded the healing of the blind man named Bartimaeus. When our pastor read the verse which says, "And Jesus said unto [the blind man], Go thy way; thy faith has made thee whole,"[3] I experienced a feeling of great excitement inside and this continued all through the fairly long sermon that followed. George Millar began to re-read Mark chapter 10, and when he got to the 52nd verse he stopped and said, "During the reading of God's Holy Word, and just at the time of the reading of this verse 52, someone received a healing in their body, praise the Lord!" and then he continued preaching. I knew then what the excitement in my body was about – God had reached down and healed me. I longed for the sermon to finish so that I could tell my husband about it, which I did immediately the service closed. I wanted to tell George that I had been healed, but there were too many people around him. However, I did get to tell his wife, and she told me to see my doctor and get proof of my healing.

---

[3] Mark 10:52 (KJV).

I was due for an injection during that week, but I felt so well – no tiredness, no feeling washed out – and I refused to attend the doctor's surgery for my injection. This continued for two or three weeks. My husband was a very 'doubting Thomas' and every day he looked for the return of my symptoms. Eventually I felt I ought to go and tell the doctor what had happened. We discussed the whole event and then the doctor said, "I want you to wait two more months and then have some blood tests done," which I did – and guess what? *No pernicious anaemia,* praise God! Well, it didn't surprise me because I knew what I had experienced was for real. God had done for me what he had done for the blind man – faith had also made me whole.

How I've praised the Lord since then and thanked him over and over for his miracle in my life, but I experienced an even more marvellous miracle when at the age of thirteen years I gave my life to Jesus and he forgave me and made me a child of his eternal Father. This is a miracle every living person is guaranteed to receive if only they will accept Jesus and his dying on the cross as their substitute for their sinful life; it's the greatest and most wonderful miracle of all.

My mother passed away on 17th April 2011, aged eighty-six and still free of pernicious anaemia.

Of course, miracles can also take place in areas other than healings and I will be recounting some which either I experienced or close friends have experienced which are simply remarkable.

Healed of M.E. (Myalgic Encephalomyelitis)

I too experienced a remarkable healing which I briefly referred to in the last chapter, and I think that my mother's healing was a springboard for my own faith to believe that God could also heal me.

In January 1991, I had gastroenteritis which lasted for three weeks. It wrecked my body, and even when the diarrhoea stopped, I never seemed to gain my strength back fully. I remember two occasions when I woke in the night feeling ill, and making my way to the bathroom, I held on to the basin with my hands as my body shook uncontrollable and my knees knocked together. I thought to myself, "There's something seriously wrong with me!"

We lived in a bungalow in a field. The house had been a wreck when we had bought it back in 1986, so we had been gradually upgrading it room by room, and I had managed to turn the field into more of a manageable garden. I had to cut the grass every couple of weeks during the summer and rake it all up, but it was never a problem and kept me fit. In July 1991, I had just cut the grass with the mower on a lovely sunny afternoon, when I suddenly felt exhausted – not my arms and legs, but inside me right to my inner core.

We went on a short holiday to St Malo in France in August, and looking back at the photographs of me there with my wife and two children, I look thin and gaunt – but the worst was yet to come.

In September I started to feel very ill – exhausted, with headaches and aching joints and a reverse sleep pattern, and my body would shake for no reason at all. I decided to visit Dr Bound, the family doctor, who did a series of blood tests. Dr Bound telephoned me early one Saturday morning as we were getting ready to attend a wedding and he said that he thought I may have diabetes. I went in the following week for more tests but these came back clear. I continued to feel exhausted and I was losing weight for no apparent reason – in fact, a stone in four weeks. One night I was shaking uncontrollably and feeling so ill that my wife called the surgery, and the doctor on call, Dr Chris Monkhouse, came to see me. He gave me a sedative to help me relax and sleep. I made an appointment to see him that week and he told me that he suspected I had M.E. – myalgic encephalomyelitis, also known at the time as 'yuppie flu'.

He said that there was no treatment for this. He told me that I would have periods of feeling normal after resting and then I would have a relapse and would have to rest until I was strong enough to cope again. He was right. I ended up going to work for the morning and would come home and sleep for two hours and then go back for the afternoon and come home and sleep most of the evening; then all night I would lie awake, unable to sleep. In December that year, I was so ill that I was admitted into hospital and I had every test in the book done, from blood tests to X-rays, but after ten days I was discharged from hospital with no issues found.

In January 1992, my employers decided that I should get a second opinion, and I was flown to London to see a doctor in Harley Street where I told him my story.

"Your doctor was right," he said. "This is a classic case of M.E. There is no cure, so you will have to manage your life accordingly."

He said that around 25% of M.E. sufferers did eventually get back to 100% of their energy levels. He did not tell me what happened to the other 75%.

I continued to work and sleep, and managed my condition as best I could, but it was such a difficult time, especially for my wife who was pregnant and my two young children. Sometimes I did not have enough energy to stand up, and so I crawled on my hands and knees down the hallway to the bathroom to go to the toilet. One night I struggled to breathe – every breathe I took was an effort as I was so exhausted – and I thought to myself, "This is it. I'm not going to make it through to the morning." I actually resigned myself to the fact that at the age of thirty I was going to die. God, however, had a plan, and it was not for me to die but for me to seek his face and receive my healing.

One morning, when I had recovered some strength, I walked down the hallway of our home and stepped out on to the patio. This was the moment of 'now or never'. I shouted at the top of my voice with all the strength I could muster, "God if you heal me, I'll serve you the rest of my days." I fell on my knees and wept and wept until there were no tears left.

Two weeks later, I managed to go to church with my family and I sat at the back of the church in case I needed to leave early through exhaustion. Guest minister Pastor Denis Phillips from Swansea was preaching, and because I felt so ill, I did not hear a word of what he said. Then he invited anyone who would like prayer to come forward. I stood up and made my way to the front of the church, holding on to the chairs at the end of each row to steady myself as my legs were so weak. When I reached the front, I stood there and Pastor Denis took my hands in his; then, in a soft, gentle voice, he prayed that I would be healed in the name of Jesus.

I fell backwards and was caught by someone and laid out on the carpet. As I lay there, I immediately felt waves of energy flowing from my head to my feet, and I thought to myself, "God is healing me!" After a while I stood up by myself without a struggle, and I walked confidently back to my family feeling absolutely amazing. I said to Bev, my wife, "I think I've been healed."

The next day I went to work and worked a full day feeling strong and full of energy, and by the end of the week I was working overtime.

Two weeks later, I thought I had better go back and see Dr Chris Monkhouse, who had been seeing me for almost a year. I walked into his consultation room, and when he saw me, he asked, "What's happened to you?"

I told him that God had healed me and I was feeling great. He was not a believer but said, "Sometimes things like this happen that we can't explain, but I'm so pleased for you."

I have never to this day had another symptom of M.E. My healing was instant, complete and permanent; I began a new adventure with God from that day forward and have never looked back.

Healing Our Land

In 2 Chronicles 7:14, God says:

> ...if my people, who are called by my name, will humble themselves and pray and seek my face and turn from their wicked ways, then I will hear from heaven, and I will forgive their sin and will heal their land.

It was around 1970, and my father was growing tomatoes in our greenhouses. When the tomatoes in the greenhouse behind our family home started to form, my father realised that there was a serious problem with them. They were all growing out of shape. In addition, the leaves were also twisted out of shape. It was soon apparent that all the tomatoes in that greenhouse, a third of his tomato harvest, were unsaleable. He called the Guernsey Horticultural Laboratory, and some men came down to analyse the crops and take soil samples. Their tests showed that weedkiller had somehow seeped into the ground and they said that he would never be able to grow crops in that ground again. A few years later, of course, tomatoes were grown in peat bags, but in those days they were grown directly in the soil. My father phoned Pastor Tony Downes, who was the pastor of the Vazon Elim Church at the time, and he came and walked up and down the greenhouse praying for a healing of the soil.

In faith my father planted the tomato seedlings in the soil the following year. Every plant grew perfectly with perfectly shaped tomatoes and perfectly shaped leaves except for six plants right by the door. It was as if God was reminding us as we walked in the door of the greenhouse that he had performed a miracle and how the crop could have been if he had not healed our land. But he did, and it was truly a miracle and an answer to prayer.

Miracle Over Nature

In the mid 1990s, a group from the church used to meet in our home to pray each Saturday night and then go together in the church minibus to various car parks around the Island of Guernsey to talk with groups of young people, who would gather regularly in certain areas, and get them into conversation about Jesus. Sometimes we had a less than friendly reception, but more often than not they were happy to talk with us. I think it broke up the boredom of their evening.

One Saturday evening, we gathered in our lounge as usual, and it had been raining all day. In fact, as we were praying, we could hear the rain pounding on the roof. We knew that no one was going to be out on a night like this.

My friend Richard started to pray and then he said in a voice of authority, "In the name of Jesus, I command you, rain, to stop."

The sound of pounding rain on the roof stopped immediately. We looked at each other amazed!

We jumped into the minibus and drove to one of the carparks, where we found a group of young people who had also come out since the rain had stopped. There we had some fruitful conversations with them about Jesus Christ.

There was a similar occasion when I was pastoring at the Kilsyth Church of God in Scotland. We had planned to have a party in the park, on what was known as 'Burn Green', and so much time and effort had been spent on making stalls and games; we had rented a marquee and made food, and had advertised it around Kilsyth.

On the Saturday morning of the event, it was raining. A member of the church who was a farmer had driven his huge trailer down to the church in the rain. We were considering whether or not to cancel the event. He walked into the church and said, "God's going to stop the rain for us; c'mon, let's load up the trailer."

So in faith we began to load all the equipment on board. As we arrived at Burn Green, the rain stopped and the sun came out, and suddenly crowds of people started arriving. Two hours later, a few minutes before the end of the event, the rain started again, and by the time we were back at church unloading, it was pouring; but during the whole time that we had held the party, there had not been a drop of rain.

How many times do we forget that God is sovereign and Jesus still has authority over the elements, and that miracles can still happen?

4

Dreams and Visions

In Acts chapter 2, on the Day of Pentecost, Peter, filled with the Holy Spirit, stood up in the streets of Jerusalem and said this:

'These people are not drunk, as you suppose. It's only nine in the morning! No, this is what was spoken by the prophet Joel:

'"In the last days, God says,
I will pour out my Spirit on all people.
Your sons and daughters will prophesy,
your young men will see visions,
your old men will dream dreams.
Even on my servants, both men and women,
I will pour out my Spirit in those days,
and they will prophesy."'

Acts 2:15-18

Having a prophetic dream or a vision from God outlining what is about to happen, or having a dream or a vision from God which is a 'word of knowledge' concerning something that has already happened, is not something that was new at

23

Pentecost, but in fact was a gift of the Holy Spirit given to many of the Old Testament prophets. We can think of Daniel who had a prophetic dream in Daniel 7, a prophetic vision in Daniel 8, an angelic visitation in Daniel 9 and a vision in Daniel 10. These dreams and visions were giving him insights into what was going to happen in the future.

In 2 Kings 6:8-12 we read this:

> *Now the king of Aram was at war with Israel. After conferring with his officers, he said, 'I will set up my camp in such and such a place.'*

> *The man of God sent word to the king of Israel: 'Beware of passing that place, because the Arameans are going down there.' So the king of Israel checked on the place indicated by the man of God. Time and again Elisha warned the king, so that he was on his guard in such places.*

> *This enraged the king of Aram. He summoned his officers and demanded of them, 'Tell me! Which of us is on the side of the king of Israel?'*

> *'None of us, my lord the king,' said one of his officers, 'but Elisha, the prophet who is in Israel, tells the king of Israel the very words you speak in your bedroom.'*

We don't know whether Elijah had dreams or visions, but certainly he had 'words of knowledge' here about the plans of the king of Aram.

This type of spiritual insight is invaluable for anyone who is in church ministry. I would like to give some accounts of dreams and visions that I have experienced which either gave me insight into what had happened in the past, or what was about to happen, or what needed to happen.

The Six Stones

It was 20th July 1995. My wife Bev and I had decided to catch the ferry from St Peter Port in Guernsey to St Malo in France and drive to St Raphael in the south of France. Ordinarily this would seem like a fairly doable journey, but we had our ten-year-old son and eight-year-old and three-year-old daughters in the car with us – who, to be fair, were incredibly well behaved and patient as we made that epic 760-mile journey down through Lyon and to the Mediterranean.

We arrived at the Key Camp site where we had hired a caravan for the week, before driving back up to Disneyland Paris and then back to St Malo to get the ferry home on 5th August.

The weather was glorious and the sun so hot that we spent much of our time in the swimming pool. One afternoon, back at the caravan, my son lay on the seat with the electric fan pointed directly at him to stay cool. I walked from the living room area of the caravan through the narrow hallway to the main bedroom, and as I entered the room I had a vision.

I stood in the room and saw in front of me a river running through a desert. The image of the river became larger and I could see a field of fruit trees planted next to the river with irrigation canals running along each row of fruit trees, but there was no water in the trenches and the trees were dying for lack of water. I looked to the river again, and where the canal connected to the river, where the water should have been flowing into the trenches, there was a pile of six large stones or rocks, and on each stone was a word. The first word was

25

'Pride', the second stone had the word 'Criticism' on it, the third had the word 'Rebellion', then 'Fear', and 'Unbelief', and finally 'Lack of Love'.

I heard the Holy Spirit say to me, "These are the six things that are stopping the flow of blessing into your church – clear the stones and the blessing will flow again, and the trees will produce fruit once more."

The vision ended.

I walked over to the bed and sat down in shock, realising that God had just revealed to me the six areas that needed addressing at my home church.

Then I heard the Holy Spirit say to me in my mind, "Continue to read Isaiah and you will receive the confirmation that what you have seen is from God."

I had been reading Isaiah, a chapter a day, and had got to chapter 24. So I grabbed my bible and began to read from chapter 25 verse 1. This is what I found:

Pride – Isaiah 25:11 (RSV):

And he will spread out his hands in the midst of it as a swimmer spreads his hands out to swim; but the LORD will lay low his pride together with the skill of his hands.

Criticism – Isaiah 29:24 (RSV):

And those who err in spirit will come to understanding, and those who murmur will accept instruction.

Rebellion – Isaiah 30:1 (RSV):

"Woe to the rebellious children," says the LORD, *"who carry out a plan, but not mine; and who make a league, but not of my spirit, that they may add sin to sin..."*

Fear – Isaiah 35:4 (RSV):

Say to those who are of a fearful heart, "Be strong, fear not!"

Unbelief – Isaiah 53:1 (RSV):

Who has believed what we have heard?

Lack of love – Isaiah 60:14 (RSV):

The sons of those who oppressed you shall come bending low to you; and all who despised you shall bow down at your feet...

I stopped reading and was about to grab a pen and write this down when I heard the Holy Spirit say, "Carry on reading." So I read through chapter 61, and then when I came across Isaiah 62:10 (RSV), I could not believe my eyes as I read:

Go through, go through the gates, prepare the way for the people; build up, build up the highway, clear it of stones...

"Clear the stones" were the words I had heard the Holy Spirit say in my mind after seeing the vison.

I shared what had happened with my wife Bev, later when the children were asleep, and we were convinced that God had revealed this whilst we were away on holiday resting because that is when God could get my attention.

Once back in Guernsey, I visited the pastor and told him what I had seen and heard and the confirmation I had received from the Word of God, and he agreed that these were the issues that needed to be addressed in the church. Often, when God speaks clearly into a situation, what you are told must be communicated wisely and carefully in order that God can change hearts and change situations. These six stones were six strongholds and each one needed to be torn down so that the water of blessing could flow again.

This was not the first vision that I had received. When we are baptised in the Holy Spirit and we are fully yielded, willing to be used by him and 'in tune' with him, anything can happen.

This same Holy Spirit came upon prophets, priests and kings in the Old Testament. This same Holy Spirit gave dreams to Joseph, visions to Isaiah and interpretation of dreams to Daniel. Anyone who is filled with the Holy Spirit can receive visions and dreams, but these always have a purpose to them and, if you receive words of knowledge, prophecy or some spiritual insight, it is not to give credence to your ministry, or to elevate you in the eyes of others, but is actually a burden of responsibility given to you for a purpose; the ultimate purpose is always to benefit the kingdom and give glory to God.

The Sailing Ship

The first vision I received was shortly after I was baptised in the Holy Spirit. I had already given an interpretation of a message in tongues one Sunday morning and now, as I was sitting in a prayer meeting in January 1994, I suddenly saw a vision of an old sailing ship on a very calm sea. I imagined that it would look like this in the doldrums. There was no wind at all, the sails in the rigging were tied up and the ship was going nowhere. Then I heard a voice in my mind say, "Let out the sails and get ready, for the wind is coming."

I assumed that God was telling me that the wind of the Holy Spirit was about to blow and the sailing ship represented our church so we needed to be ready for it. I told my pastor about it and he agreed that we needed a fresh wind of the Holy Spirit in the church.

What I did not know was that on 20th January something extraordinary happened in a church in Toronto which soon spread across the world – something called the 'Toronto Blessing'.

I first heard about it a few weeks later on the BBC news, when there was a report of churches in the UK experiencing this phenomenon of people falling on the floor laughing and barking like dogs. When Bev and I heard this, we turned to each other astonished and started to discuss it, questioning how on earth that could be of God. Then Wynne Lewis, the General Superintendent of the Elim Movement, came over to the Island for a joint meeting of the churches at Delancey Elim Church, and as he prayed for people, they were being 'slain in the Spirit', laughing and crying, and it was an incredible evening. I had seen people slain in the Spirit before back in the early 1970s in our new church building, where I remember that there was not enough carpet space to lay everyone down on when they were prayed for.

Bev has an entry in her diary on 3rd March 1994 simply saying, "Slain in the Spirit."

Our church, however, never really experienced any of this phenomenon, although we had a home group at our house where we would stand and hold each other's shoulders, and one by one would experience a powerful anointing and would fall to the floor laughing until it hurt.

I was travelling to Newcastle for business that year and took a taxi in the evening to the Sunderland Christian Centre, which was built in the middle of a rough housing estate. There was a high wire fence around the car park to stop people stealing the cars whilst people were in the services, which were held almost every night. The meeting was excellent and I sensed a powerful presence of the Holy Spirit. I was about to leave when someone asked if they could pray for me, and I was soon 'slain in the Spirit' on the floor. After some time, I managed to get up and, walking into the foyer, I asked someone on the desk if there was a taxi rank nearby. The lady kindly said that there was but I could be attacked walking there at that time of night. A couple of men next to me asked where I was going and I said, "Newcastle." They then offered to drop me off as they were from Fraserburgh in Scotland and were making their way home via Newcastle in their transit van. So I made it back to my hotel opposite Newcastle train station in one piece. I really believe that God arranged my safe passage back.

I also attended a Rodney Howard-Browne meeting in Olympia in London with my friends Andrew and Georgina that year. Having been prayed for by Paula and Randy White, and having spent some time on the carpet, we made our way home, down towards Earls Court, as I danced down the pavement. For any of you who know me, that was totally out of character!

On 29th September the following year, I had been working in New York all week and had decided to fly home via Toronto. I arrived at the Airport Hotel in Toronto and immediately made my way on foot to the Airport Vineyard church, where the

'Toronto Blessing' had begun. I walked into the church foyer and immediately sensed the presence of the Holy Spirit.

My experience of the 'Toronto Blessing' changed my life and released me into a deeper walk with the Holy Spirit. I believe that the vision of the sailing ship and the message about the wind about to blow was concerning this global move of the Holy Spirit. Sadly, I do not think that the church was fully ready for that fresh wind to blow.

How important it is when God reveals something to you that you take heed of it.

The Hour of Intercession

I was getting ready to go to bed one evening and it was around 10.30pm. I had locked all the doors and put the kitchen light off; then, just as I was leaving the lounge, I felt compelled by the Holy Spirit to pray. I told Bev and she went on to bed and left me to spend time in prayer.

I had no idea what I was to pray for, so I started to pray in tongues. I was walking the length of the room praying in tongues, then turning around and walking back the length of the room, and I continued like this, praying in tongues, doing spiritual warfare, but with no clue as to what or who I was interceding for. This continued for about an hour, and then I suddenly stopped and knew that whatever it was, it was done. I made my way to the bedroom, and as I did so, I saw in my mind's eye the face of Pastor Eric Gaudion. I knew that he had been unwell with pancreatitis and thought that perhaps I was praying for him because he needed prayer right there and then. I got into the bed and fell asleep, and I did not give the incident another thought.

A few months later, I bumped into Eric, and remembering the incident, I told him about it. He asked me when it was that I had felt led to intercede in prayer, and when I told him, he said that it was the night before a major operation that he was due to have and that I was not the first person to say that they had been prompted by the Holy Spirit to pray that night. It was possible that the enemy had had intentions for evil during that operation and yet God had prompted me and others to intercede for him that night. How important it is for us, when the Holy Spirit speaks, to obey.

A Man on a Plane

I used to fly from Guernsey to London several times a year to meet with law firms, accountants and clients when I worked in banking and finance. In 1996 I had planned to visit my clients in London when Rodney Howard-Browne was ministering at Wembley Arena. So after a day of client meetings, I made my way to the meeting. The following day, I took the Gatwick Express to the airport and made my way to the departure lounge. It was a full flight and all the seats in the lounge were occupied. A few years earlier, I had read John Wimber's book, *Power Evangelism*, and had been inspired by his story of his plane flight when he saw the word 'Adultery' on a man's face. Obviously, it wasn't actually written on his face, but the Holy Spirit was giving John a word of knowledge about the man. If you've read the story, you will know that he arranged to talk to him and the man repented. I never thought that I would ever have a similar encounter on a plane.

As I sat in the lounge, I looked at the man in a suit sitting opposite me. He had long, blond hair and looked more like a rock star than a businessman. I was to discover that he was indeed a bass player in a rock band.

As I looked at him, the Holy Spirit said to me, "Talk to him."

I said to the Holy Spirit, that voice in my head, "Pardon?"

The voice came back again, "Talk to him."

I said, "How can I talk to him? I can't shout across the room and there's no free seat next to him." I thought for a moment and then said to the Holy Spirit, "If he sits next to me on the plane, I will talk to him."

Boarding was announced, and I made my way on to the plane and found my seat. People were queueing to get on as usual and, of course, the inevitable happened: the man with the long, blond hair sat next to me. I had no clue as to why I had to speak to him, there was no word written across his face! So I thought that I had better start the conversation straight away.

I said, "Hi there. I'm Mike."

He shook my hand and said, "I'm George."

I then said to him, "Are you visiting Guernsey or do you work there?"

George said that he worked in Guernsey and that he was a town planner working for the Island Development Committee.

I said to George, "Ah, I know Andy Shilling who drafts policies for your department." Then I added, "But he is leaving soon to go to Bible college."

George looked at me with a quizzical smile on his face and asked, "Are you a Christian?"

Maybe it was because I had used the term 'Bible college' in a positive way. I said that I was and then he began to share his story with me. He told me how he was a backslidden Christian. He used to attend a local Baptist church in Guernsey but playing in a local rock band had drawn him away from church, although his wife and children still attended each week. He told me how much he loved and admired his wife for her strong faith and how he regretted the fact that he had walked away from God. Before we landed, he said to me, "That was no accident that we sat together today; I'm definitely going to get back on track with God." I did not tell him about the Holy Spirit's prompting and how God had arranged this!

A few years later, I was running a youth café and had invited my good friend Glenn to come and sing. He brought a bass player with him – George!

A few years ago, I wanted to tell this story, so I did a Google search to try and find George's contact details, to see if he was OK with me sharing this. Sadly, I saw that he had passed away from cancer on 10th June 2012. It dawned on me that the Holy Spirit wanted to speak to George through me to give him an opportunity to get his life right with God.

How important it is to be listening to the Holy Spirit and to be obedient when he speaks to you.

You may be thinking that I am a person who is always in tune with the Holy Spirit and that I always get it right. Let me tell you about a time when I was *not* listening.

A Flight from Miami to New York

In 2007 I was attending a two-day tax conference in Miami with some other senior directors of Deutsche Bank. I found the conference rather tedious and boring. I was so glad to board the plane to New York, where we would be holding some meetings with the Latin America relationship managers before flying back to Guernsey.

I found my seat on the plane in the business class section and was looking forward to sleeping during the three-hour flight. As I was getting my iPod ready and earphones to listen to some relaxing music during the flight, a man sat down next to me and smiled and said hello. He then asked me if I was going to use the blanket I had been given, and I said no, he could have it. Then, as soon as the plane was in the air, I switched on my music and drifted off to sleep.

I heard the announcement saying that we would shortly be landing so I sat up and switched off my music. As the plane came in to land on the runway, the man next to me thanked me for the blanket. He told me that he got cold as he was going through chemotherapy and was flying to New York to see his cancer doctor. They had only given him a few months to live.

The plane came to a standstill and I realised, to my shame, that God had put me next to this man to talk to him, not to sleep, and I had just missed a God-given opportunity because I was not listening to the Holy Spirit. Hopefully, I have learnt from this mistake – and many others that I have made. I do not want to look back on my life and regret missed opportunities like this, but rather rejoice in the ones I have been given and have been obedient in.

The Hooded Men and a Curse on the Church

Joel prophesied, "It shall come to pass in the last days, says God, that I will pour out of my Spirit on all flesh; your sons and your daughters shall prophesy, your young men shall see visions, your old men shall dream dreams."

I have had 'words of knowledge' through visions and dreams and they have come at crucial times, when it was imperative for me to know what was happening, or what had happened, and then act accordingly.

It was 2006, and I had just finished three years of pastoring my first church and was now working as an associate pastor with Pastor John Roddis at the Delancey Elim Church in Guernsey.

The church was struggling somewhat, and although we were working hard and trying anything and everything to see people saved, nothing was happening. We sat in John's office one morning and were praying for a breakthrough. Then suddenly I had a vision.

In my vision I was lifted up out of the office and above the church and then taken over the roofs of the houses behind the church until I found myself looking at one particular house in the back lane. As I watched, it was suddenly night-time and everything was dark. The front door opened and a group of hooded people came out of the house and made their way down the road to the church and then proceeded to walk around the church chanting. It seemed obvious that these people were members of a local coven and that they were cursing the church.

Suddenly I was back in the room with Pastor John, and I shared what I had just seen in the vision. He said that we should get the church leaders together and tell them, and pray against the curse. When they arrived that evening, I suggested that we walk around the church building and break the curse in Jesus' name, so we did. As I walked, in my mind I could hear the sweeping of a brush. Then I remembered what Jesus had said in Matthew 12:43-44:

> *When an impure spirit comes out of a person, it goes through arid places seeking rest and does not find it. Then it says, "I will return to the house I left." When*

it arrives, it finds the house unoccupied, swept clean and put in order.

The sweeping sound was the removal of the curse on the church.

Almost immediately we saw new people coming to church, and many made decisions to follow Jesus – in fact, twenty-two new converts in the following six months.

This insight into what had happened was key to the church moving forward. I wonder how many churches are experiencing lack of fruitfulness due to curses placed on them by covens? We must remember that the name of Jesus can break every chain, every curse, and everything that is named must bow to his name. We have all authority to destroy the work of the evil one, and if we identify a stronghold we are more than able to tear it down.

A Family Curse by a Juju Man

In 2010 I was on team, pastoring a church in Chelmsford, and a lady from Nigeria had asked to see me. She said that her family back home were having a terrible time with many sick and some had died. She asked if I could pray for her and her family, which I agreed to do.

As we bowed our heads to pray, I suddenly had a vision. It was as if I had been taken from the room we were in to a village in Nigeria. I saw a corrugated iron hut, and in my mind's eye I saw a person walking to the back of the house, past a chicken wire fence, and through the gate to the back door, which was painted red. The person knocked on the door and a man opened it. The person handed money to the man and then left.

I told the lady what I had seen and she said that she knew the house – it was the house of the Juju man in her village and that someone must have paid him to put a curse on her family. So with this knowledge, we began to pray with power and authority, binding the curse and turning it back from where it came.

The Blue Flower Vase

We were worshipping one Sunday morning at a church, when in the middle of the worship I had a vision. I saw a young boy and then I saw a blue flower vase fall off a table and smash on the floor. It seemed a bit bizarre and I had no idea why the Holy Spirit was showing me this. However, I have learnt not to question the Holy Spirit but simply to obey him.

I got up after the worship and told the church what I had seen and said something like, "God saw that incident. As a result of what happened, the boy was punished and suffered greatly. God wants to bring healing of that memory."

No one came to me after the service to say anything.

It was the following week that a man in his fifties said, "That was me. It was a blue flower vase and my mother broke it, but when my father got home later that day, drunk, he blamed me and beat me."

The man then gave me further details of abuse that followed for years after that incident.

I was able to refer him for some deep spiritual counselling, and after a week away he returned, feeling that the painful memories of what had been done to him had finally been healed.

I realise that, sadly, a large number of men and women who have been abused as children carry a huge burden on their shoulders throughout their lives; even when they come to Christ, there isn't necessarily an immediate release from the hurt and damage caused in their childhood. God's love is such that he desires not just to save a soul, but to bring healing and wholeness to a person. 'Words of knowledge' can reveal the hurts, and then the deep-rooted issues can be addressed.

I wrote a poem about this incident. If you can identify with the subject, then take heart; God is on your case and he loves you so deeply that he doesn't want you to carry the hurt any longer.

A broken vase on the floor
A shout of rage, a slamming door
A fist, a punch, a drunken brawl
I cover my eyes, back to the wall
I only wish the pain would cease
Abused and confused, I long for peace
Body shaking, tears streaking, pain searing, voices
    shrieking
The cuts will heal and bruises will fade
But my life is scarred and a price has been paid
Walking wounded through my life
Each kick, each hand, each stick, each knife
Will my future be determined by the wounds and
    the scars?
Will I always live within these prison bars?

Jesus answers:
I was pierced and bruised and in pain
So that you could find healing in my name
On Calvary's cross my love for you was revealed

> *And today, my child, by my stripes you can be*
> *healed.*

A Girl in a Red Dress

A church that I was pastoring seemed on the surface to be ticking along nicely, with a large group of teenagers and a growing number of people attending – everything a pastor could hope for. However, as I was praying in tongues walking around the inside of the church one day, I sensed something not of God in an area of the room. I was walking up one aisle, around past the media desk and down the other aisle, and there was a chair under the window facing inwards. I sensed in my spirit that there was a demonic being, literally sitting on that seat. I felt that it had been there for many years and was a spirit of lust.

When I had 'preached with a view' at the church on a Sunday morning during the interview process, I had left the building after the service and my wife had said to me, "What do you think?"

I said to her, "It's a great church but there's a spirit of lust in there."

Now, some ten or eleven months after arriving, I was sensing this spirit haughtily opposing me as I prayed. I opened the door into the foyer and the door outside, then I came back and stood by the media desk which was alongside the foyer door. I began to speak to this invisible being sitting on the chair and commanded it to leave the building in the name and authority given to me by Jesus Christ. For about ten minutes, I spoke out against this spirit. Then, suddenly, I felt it rise up and walk past me, brushing so close to me that the hairs on my neck stood up, after which it was gone.

I took the anointing oil and put oil on the doorframes of the church and prayed that it would never again return.

Almost immediately sexual sins started coming to the surface. A man called me and said that he had to see me right away. I had a migraine and tried to put him off, but he insisted that it was urgent. He arrived at the house and sat in my lounge, and told me that he had been texting a young girl in the church and that he had foolishly been saying some things that he should not as a married man. I said that he needed to tell his wife and that the girl should tell her parents, as she was just seventeen and living at home.

That night I had a dream. In my dream I saw this young woman at the age of between eight and ten in a red dress, and behind her was a corrugated wall of a barn or shed. She was with an older man, but I could not see his face. The dream ended but I knew what had transpired: she had been sexually abused.

My wife and I had this young woman at our home to talk to her, and she confirmed that she had been sexually abused when she was young but would not say who the older man was.

And so the unravelling began. Without going into detail, we slowly uncovered a network of sexual immorality in the church. I say 'slowly' because there were so many lies told by so many people that it took months to uncover the truth.

I began to research past sexual issues in the church and it went back many years. How long the spirit of lust had been a stronghold in the church, I do not know, but I do know that once it was gone, all the secret sins were revealed.

It came to a point that although I could not tell the church everything, I had to deal with the issue once and for all, so as I prayer-walked one day, the Holy Spirit made it clear what I should do. I went and borrowed the 'Churches Together' cross, which we carried through the town on a Good Friday, and placed it in the centre of the platform where I would normally preach, and I instead preached from the side. I spoke that Sunday morning on the 'woman caught in adultery' and the seriousness of sexual sin. Then I said something like, "There is sexual sin in this church and it cannot continue. This is an opportunity for repentance. So if you want to surrender afresh to Christ, why don't you come and kneel at the cross…" I then added, "I haven't been involved in sexual sin, but I will be the first to kneel to ensure that my life is right before God."

I went and knelt before the cross, and I could hear a scuffling behind me. When I looked, two thirds of the church were on their knees.

Almost immediately we started to see people saved in their ones and twos, something we had not seen since I had started pastoring that church.

How I thank God for the revelation he gave me through a prophetic dream.

Get Up and Preach – This is Your Church

It was Saturday, 25th March 2017. During the night, I had a dream. I was standing by a platform of a church. The church was large and mainly blacked out, like a Hillsong church. I watched as the worship team were getting ready to start the service. Hundreds of people were milling around and standing talking to each other in the congregation. I looked past the worship team and saw a choir, and said to myself, "A choir. That's unusual in this day and age." Then I heard a voice behind me say, "Get up and preach – this is your church." I woke up and told Bev about the dream.

She said, "Maybe God's got a new church lined up for you and was preparing you."

On Tuesday, 18th April, just over three weeks later, I received a phone call from the senior pastor from my previous church. He said that he was caretaking a church in Essex, as they were in between pastors, and asked whether Bev and I would come and do a teaching weekend for him – and would I preach on the Sunday morning? I agreed and then I went on the internet and looked the church up. To my surprise, there was the church that I had dreamt about, and on the platform was the choir that I had seen in my dream.

We went down on the weekend of 2nd July, and on the Saturday I did some teaching on small group networks and Bev did a ladies' event. Then on the Sunday morning I preached to about four hundred people, and three people responded to the gospel. I knew that this was where God wanted me to be.

However, when I applied for the position of Pastor the following January, it took ages before I could be interviewed. Having made the final three, I was totally confident that God had opened the door and had already formulated great plans for growing the church. The Regional Leader had recommended me, saying that I had experience of a larger church environment at Life Church in Chelmsford and my background in banking and finance would be ideal for a larger church. But on Sunday, 5th August, I received an email saying that I had been turned down.

I struggled with this for many months as I knew clearly that God wanted me to be the pastor at that church. I questioned why, if it was right, it had not happened.

I was praying much about this, and then one day the prophet Daniel came to mind. God revealed to me that instead of sitting back and expecting God to just sort it out for me as it was his will anyway, I should have immediately fasted and prayed until God's will was done. There was a battle in the heavenlies to be fought and won. I learnt my lesson, but I do wonder sometimes what could have happened if I had been appointed as the pastor and what great things God had planned for that church.

The Family Reconciliation

One morning I had finished preaching at the church in Chelmsford and I had invited people to come forward for prayer. I was praying for one lady and sensed that the Holy Spirit was telling me to prophesy about healing and recon-ciliation for her and her family. I did not know her family situation at all. Apparently, her relationship with her sister had broken down and they had not spoken for many years. In 2014 she messaged me to say that they had reconciled. She said in her message:

> Only God could restore the years the locust has eaten. We're getting to know each other again. Thank you for being obedient to Jesus and saying that prophecy in Elim all those years ago.

Then, on 22nd September 2019, she said this:

> God has done so much healing in our relationship and it just keeps on getting better. Thanks so much for being obedient and hearing God with your prophetic message when you were at Elim. It gave me hope that one day we would be reconciled. I have my sister back and it's all Jesus' work

through the power of the Holy Spirit and using you, his servant.

God is a God of reconciliation, and if we listen closely to what the Holy Spirit is saying, anything is possible.

5

Discernment and Deliverance Ministry

The Dark Cloud in a Lady's Home

I never imagined that I would ever become a pastor. My journey into ministry probably began when I made the decision to go part-time for the bank and utilise my afternoons assisting Pastor Paul Gower in door-to-door ministry. He mentored me in preaching and teaching, visiting the sick and every other aspect of ministry.

Then on Thursday, 21st November 2002, the Elim Regional Leader, Mike Epton, came across to Guernsey and met with Bev and me at our home; he asked if I would consider becoming the pastor of the Patria Christian Fellowship in Guernsey. I felt convinced that this was what God wanted me to do, so I said yes.

On Wednesday, 4th December, I met with the Patria church members and they agreed to my appointment.

One member asked me, "Do you know what you're taking on?" I said that I did but I really did not!

On Sunday, 26th January 2003, I was inducted as Pastor of Patria Church.

It turned out that there were only twenty members when I took the first service. We met in a community centre and had to set up all the chairs and the overhead projector; I had to help lead worship as well as preach, and as the youth club leaders had also left, I had to run the youth club too with my wife and daughter and a few other helpers from other churches, and even a colleague or two from the bank.

We immediately began to produce and distribute a newsletter around the parish, splitting into twos and walking through the lanes and estates putting these through people's letterboxes. We actually printed off 1,500 church magazines on A3 paper on an inkjet printer at home!

As a result of several distributions, one farmer came along to the church and gave his life to Christ.

However, the true impact of the magazine distribution only became apparent three years later when I had left the Patria church and was appointed as Associate Pastor to the Delancey Elim Church in the north of the Island. I received a phone call on my mobile from a lady who had received a church magazine through her door and had put it in a drawer in her living room.

She lived on a fairly new estate and had put her house on the market for sale because every evening a dark cloud descended in her living room and there was the sound of chains being dragged along the floor upstairs. Her daughter was so scared that she was living at a friend's house. The lady was a Christian and had opened her drawer, found the church magazine, and in desperation called my mobile number which was on the church contact details. She asked me if I could help her.

I spoke to John Roddis, who was the senior pastor at the Delancey Church, and he agreed to come with me to pray in the lady's house.

I called her and arranged a convenient time, and we headed up to her home, which was near the airport.

Walking into the house, we did not sense anything evil, so we just walked around all the rooms and commanded any demon or evil presence to leave in the name of Jesus. We took turns to read scriptures in each room which declared the goodness and power of God.

After talking again with the lady, we left.

Two weeks later, she called me again and said that since we had prayed in the house, the dark cloud had not appeared again and there was no longer the sound of chains being dragged along the floor upstairs. The house felt at peace. Her daughter had moved back in and she had taken the house off the market.

This was the first experience for me of cleansing a home of an evil spirit.

The Demon with Glowing Red Eyes

A while later I was called by a young man whom I had been counselling. He lived on the Bouet estate in Guernsey, an area of housing which was run-down and housed some of the poorest families. He himself had been in prison and had come from a troubled family. I had taught him guitar and, in fact, I had given him one of my guitars, as he had very little money. He was calling me about a young mother on the estate whom he knew. She was a single mum with three children and she lived in a two-bedroom council flat. One of her young sons kept waking up in the night screaming, seeing a being in his room with glowing red eyes. Pastor John was away, so I called my friend Pastor Steve Mudge and we went together to the estate.

The young man took us to the flat, and it broke my heart to see the conditions that this young mum was living in. There was no carpet in the hallway, just a concrete floor, and in the living room there was a large burnt area in the middle of the carpet where one of the boys had lit a fire. There was black mould on her living room ceiling. Steve and I prayed in each room and commanded any demon or evil spirit to leave in the name of Jesus, and we read some scriptures too.

I talked to the young mum and told her that just as she could see that evil existed, so did God, and he loved her and her boys; in a simple way, I shared the gospel with her. It was such a joy and a privilege a few weeks later to baptise her in water as she started coming to the church and gave her life to Jesus. From that day, her young son slept right through the night every night, with no more waking up and no more sights of things with glowing red eyes.

I could not leave that young mum living in such squalor. My employers were replacing the carpet squares in the banking hall and throwing out the old ones which were perfectly good, so I asked if I could have them. I filled my car with a hundred or so carpet squares and took them to her flat. There was a carpet layer in the church, so after a team of us had cleaned and painted her flat, he went and took away the burnt carpet and laid these tiles throughout the hallway and the living room.

A while later this young mum called me and said that the flat next to her had been broken into and the woman in the flat had been raped. She was terrified that harm could come to her and her boys.

I wrote to the housing authority on her behalf and asked if it was possible for her to move to another estate where she could have a three-bedroom flat or house, and almost immediately she was allocated a beautiful three-bedroom home on another estate nearer to the town of St Peter Port.

I had asked a couple in the church, whose two boys had grown up, if they would consider being a spiritual mum and dad to her, and they were delighted to do so, even babysitting for her so she could go to evening class and train as a secretary. They also helped her with cooking, and the reward for us was when she invited both this couple and me and my wife to her new council house and she cooked us a beautiful meal that she had prepared.

There is no greater joy than witnessing a life transformed by the power of God.

The Spirit of Suicide

Whilst still at the Delancey church, a lovely Christian lady who attended the church spoke to me one Sunday morning after the service and said that a neighbour of hers was very troubled as she kept waking up in the night choking, feeling that an invisible hand was around her throat. I agreed to come to meet her and pray in her home.

On Thursday, 8th May 2008, I went to the address, and the lady introduced her neighbour to me. I went into the house and into the bedroom and began to pray and then command any demon or evil presence to leave in the name of Jesus. As I came out of the bedroom, the two ladies were on the landing. I asked her which room was next door to her bedroom; she said that it was her son's room. I asked if I could pray in there too and she agreed, so I entered the room and shut the door. Immediately I sensed the presence of an evil spirit. I commanded it to leave in the name of Jesus, and as I did so, the Holy Spirit told me that it was the spirit of suicide. I left the room and told the lady that I had sensed the presence of a spirit of suicide in that room. The lady was shocked and said that her son's father had committed suicide. It seemed that the same spirit that had pressured his father to take his life was now trying to influence the boy too and was also trying to take the wife's life by strangling her in the night.

I received a call from my church member a few days later saying that the lady's son, the morning after I had prayed in his room and unaware that I had done so, told his mum that his room felt really peaceful and empty! The lady had slept fine, with no more demonic attacks in the night.

The boy's stepdad, who worked at the hospital, came the following Sunday to church to hear an evangelist, who was also a qualified doctor, and he gave his life to Christ.

A Strangling Spirit

As with the lady in Guernsey, another lady approached me in our Chelmsford church with the same experience.

She was Chinese and a Christian, one of the many who came along to our Chinese church which I helped establish when I was there. We had a wonderful godly lady in the church called Helen, and I knew as soon as I met her that there was a call of God on her to be a pastor. We taught English to immigrants as a ministry in the church and, as a result, had made contact with a number of Chinese people from Hong Kong and Mainland China. Although some were not Christians, they enjoyed coming to the Chinese church services for friendship and fellowship. One couple from mainland

China had retired in England. They had both been members of the Communist Party and they said to me, through Helen interpreting, that they had "never heard of this Jesus".

That set me on a mission. I searched the internet for material to use, and found the film series 'Jesus of Nazareth' with Chinese subtitles from a Los Angeles online store and bought it. Although Cantonese and Mandarin are different when spoken, they are the same in written form, so both the people from mainland China and Hong Kong could understand the subtitles.

We ran a video each week, and when the series was over, I obtained the 'Alpha Course' with Nicky Gumbel dubbed into Chinese with subtitles too. At the end of the Alpha course, the couple from Mainland China and another lady gave their lives to Jesus.

So, back to the story of the lady from the group who was waking up in the night choking and feeling like something was strangling her...

I agreed to go to her flat and pray. On arrival, I met her and her husband, who was not a Christian, and her young daughter and young son. I went into each room to pray, and in the bathroom I sensed a spirit of suicide once again, and had an impression that someone had taken a drug overdose in that bathroom.

I commanded any demon or evil spirit to leave that bathroom and I did the same in the bedroom. I also had a word of prophecy for the young daughter, who was probably pre-teen or early teen.

The lady said that unfortunately she still continued to have the occasional sensation of being strangled in the night. The spirit was obviously in no hurry to leave that flat, and I did have a sense that something the husband was doing helped it stay put.

The Demon of Suicide Again

In Chelmsford we got to know a lovely young married couple. The young lady was having episodes of dark depression and voices in her head telling her to harm herself and even take her own life.

Bev and I visited the couple in their flat, and her husband was so stressed and concerned about his wife that he did not know what to do.

I had mentioned the situation to the senior pastor, who said that he had not really been involved in deliverance ministry as in his previous church he'd had a team that dealt with this.

Apart from the deliverance of a young man in my home in Guernsey when I was young and was told to stay in the garden, I had only read about delivering people from demons, so I was not going to conduct such a session by myself.

I contacted pastors Richard and Rajinder Buxton in our Elim Ealing church, as I knew that they had a deliverance ministry team in their church. Bev and I took this young lady in the car down to Ealing for a chat with Rajinder.

In the office, she talked about a friend of hers who was into the occult and had taken her home one day; they had levitated the settee so high that their heads were against the ceiling. Rajinder said that this was the entry point for the demon who was now telling her to harm herself.

Ealing Christian Centre held deliverance meetings once a month on a Saturday from 11am to 1pm, so we arranged to take the young lady down on a particular Saturday. She was silent all the way down in the car and her eyes were glazed over.

The church building was huge. It was formerly the Top Hat Club, and Pastor John Marriott, who used to be my pastor in Guernsey, had left Guernsey and moved to London and had purchased the building and turned it into a church; the numbers grew from a couple of hundred to over a thousand. Those requiring deliverance ministry were sitting at the front of the church, the chairs were placed about six feet apart and that morning there were about six or seven people. The team, which included Pastor Richard, began to move from person to person and they spoke directly to the evil spirits, commanding them to leave that person. There were some buckets or bowls to hand, as sometimes the person was physically sick when they were delivered. Others would spit or writhe on the floor and slither like a snake. Some would scream or shout. It was spiritual warfare in the raw. Bev and I sat behind the young lady and prayed and watched.

She sat still, not making a sound until an hour and a half had passed, when suddenly she groaned loud and long and then fell silent. 1pm came and she turned around and looked at us. Her eyes were clear and sparkling, and she started to talk and did not stop talking all the way home.

She never had another urge to harm herself and no more voices in her head. She was free. This lovely couple now have two gorgeous daughters, and I hold the whole family with deep affection.

The Internet Café

Although Guernsey sounds like an idyllic island, and in many ways it is, it has an undercurrent of witchcraft and occult practice which seems to run in families, generation after generation.

One young lady, who came to our church through working with someone from the church, made a decision for Jesus and immediately began to have horrific nightmares. She started to remember things that had happened to her in the past in her family and realised that things had been done to her as a child that could only be part of some occult ritual. She wanted to be free of the nightmares, and an elder in the church and the friend that brought her to church began to meet with her to deliver her from the demons that had been put on her as a child. At one such meeting, whilst she was six months pregnant, she ran out into the back garden and leapt over a six-foot fence, such was the power of the demonic forces in her. She was completely delivered and set free, and her husband, who had been an atheist, became a Christian on seeing and experiencing what happened to his wife.

There was an internet café in St Peter Port, and even though it was for people to use the computers to surf the net, there were many occult paraphernalia in the shop, including brochures about white witchcraft and covens that people could contact.

I was walking up the street past the shop on the way to work one morning, having parked the car on one of the piers, and I suddenly heard the Holy Spirit say to me, "Curse that shop to close." I did exactly that. There was no one else around, so as I passed, I looked at the shop front and said, "In the name of Jesus Christ, I curse you to close." I walked on, went to work at the bank and thought no more of it. A few weeks later, I was walking past the shop again on the way to work and it was shut and boarded up!

The Name of Jesus

We all know that there is power in the name of Jesus. That's because God has given Jesus...

> ...*[the] name that is above every name that at the name of Jesus every knee should bow, in heaven and on earth and under the earth, and every tongue acknowledge that Jesus Christ is Lord, to the glory of God the Father.*
>
> *Philippians 2:10-11*

It is not the name of Jesus in itself that is powerful, but the authority behind that name.

Bev and I were taking a walk through the countryside one day back in the late nineties with Pastor Des Morton and his wife. Des was the senior pastor of the Keynsham Elim Church, and we were visiting some friends who attended that church. As I walked through the country lanes, Des began to tell me a story which has stayed with me and is akin to the type of accounts I had read as a child in the book *From Witchcraft to Christ* by Doreen Irvine.

Hugh was a painter-decorator and worked for the council. He was an elder in a local church. One day he was painting in a corridor in a block of flats and happened to notice that one of the doors to a flat was ajar. He could see a woman sitting on a chair in the flat reading a bible. She looked up and saw him and smiled. He said, "Good Morning," and she returned the greeting. He then said, "Excuse me, is that a bible you are reading?"

She said, "Yes it is."

He then asked her, "Are you a Christian?"

The reply she gave made him shiver. "No," she said, "I'm a witch. I'm reading the references to witchcraft in the Bible."

Hugh thought that this was an opportunity for him to talk to her about Jesus. She invited him into the room to talk.

The more he talked about Jesus, the more agitated she became until she said, "Look, I have far more power than you will ever have and I will prove it." She stood up and went to the window. "You see that streetlight across the road?" she said. "I'm going to curse it and it will shatter into pieces."

Hugh watched as she cursed the lamp and it exploded, shards of glass cascading down on to the pavement.

"Now," she said, "I'm going to curse you and you're going to die right here in this room."

Hugh did not know whether to run or hide or stand his ground, but his heart was pounding in his chest. She started to curse him to die, and Hugh couldn't think of anything to do except shout out as loud as he could, "JESUS!" The woman fell backwards on to the floor and lay still as if dead.

Hugh was glued to the spot watching as she suddenly came to and said to him, "What just happened?" She stood to her feet and told Hugh to stay in the room; she would be back really soon. A few minutes later she returned with a man and a woman. The man was a warlock and the woman another member of the coven.

The woman from the flat said to Hugh, "We are going to prove to you that we have more power than you. We're going to curse you and you are going to die right now."

They began to curse him to die. Hugh immediately shouted out, "JESUS!" and the three of them fell backwards on the floor and lay there as if they were dead. After a few moments they scrambled to their feet with a look of shock and incredulity on their faces, and the warlock and other witch left the room in a hurry. Hugh had the privilege of leading the young woman to Christ, and once she had gone through deliverance ministry, she became an active member of the church.

I had hoped to contact Hugh for his consent to include this story in this book, but having spoken to Evangelist Hayden Morton, the nephew of Des Morton, he informed me that Hugh has now been promoted to glory, passing away in his late eighties / early nineties. Hayden was sure that both Hugh and Des would want this story to be published in order to give all the glory to Jesus, whose name is higher than any other name, and at whose name every knee shall bow!

6

Miracles of Protection

When we read the Bible, we come across many stories of how God protected people from harm. We learn how the blood of the lamb on the doorframes of the houses in Egypt provided protection for the Israelites; we see how David was protected many times by God; and in the Christmas story we hear of the Magi being warned in a dream and Joseph being warned in a dream.

There is no doubt that God has a preordained plan for our lives, even though many times we wander off track. So God will step in and protect us in order that his plan for our lives may be fulfilled. There is still free will, of course, and we do need to pray for protection because the enemy of our souls can (and will, if possible) disrupt God's plan for us. Intercessory prayer is a key to ensuring that God's will is done on earth as it is in heaven.

Let me tell you some extraordinary stories of God's protection.

A Piece of Shrapnel

My grandfather William was twenty-one years old and working as a grower in the tomato industry in Guernsey when war in Europe began in 1914.

Germany's military forces were tramping through Europe, taking country after country, but Guernsey had no compulsory military service. Many men wanted to fight, and the only way for them to do so was to enlist with the Royal Irish Regiment who were stationed at Fort Hommet, which dominated the headland to the north of Vazon Bay, on the West Coast of the Island. So William, aged twenty-two, and his older brother James made their way in 1915 to line up with many others to enlist to join the army.

On 5th March 1915, the volunteers gathered at the docks in St Peter Port, ready to sail to Ireland, where the recruits received intense training and where William was selected to operate a Vickers Portable Machine Gun.

The Regiment was based at Fermoy in Ireland until September 1915, when it moved to Blackdown Camp near Aldershot in the South of England.

Fully trained and ready to fight, the Guernsey contingent sailed from England, and on 19th December 1915, James and William, with thirty-three officers and 996 men of the 6th Royal Irish Regiment, arrived in France at Drouvin. From here parties of officers and men were attached to the 8th London Regiment (Post Office Rifles) and would go into the trenches for two days at a time for instruction.

On 26th January 1916, the first Guernsey casualties from enemy action occurred, when forty-year-old Major George Le Page was killed. A number of other men were also wounded.

During the following few weeks, many Guernsey men died in the fighting, and on 10th June 1916, after three months of intense fighting and huge losses on each side, William received the devastating news that his brother James had been killed in a trench raid just down the line from where he was stationed. James was just one of the 37,121 British soldiers killed that month alone in offensives and counter-offensives.

A month later, as William was firing the machine gun to support another advance across 'no man's land', he suddenly felt a pain in his hand. Looking down, he could see a tear through his flesh and blood pumping out over his sleeve. He had been hit and wounded by a piece of shrapnel. He was relieved of his post and taken for medical treatment.

Unable to use his hand, he was unfit for duty and was sent home to Guernsey to recover from his wound. This was just prior to the battle of the Somme which saw many of his fellow Guernseymen killed in the intensity of the fighting and the increase in gas attacks.

If my grandfather had not been wounded, I probably wouldn't be here now. Who would have thought that a small piece of shrapnel could have saved my chance to exist and the six children he went on to father, as well as the seventeen grandchildren who, all in turn, had children – some doctors, some nurses, some bank managers and some church ministers. All of our lives were held in the balance and dependent upon one small piece of shrapnel which wounded William Frederick Guille on that day in the trenches in Belgium.

Also, after recovering from his wound in Guernsey, on 9th December 1917, William married a widow called Drusilla Ferbrache who had a baby girl. She had lost her husband Lance

Corporal Wilfred Le Noury on 7th June 1917 fighting at Ypres. Drusilla was my grandmother.

A Strangulated Hernia

When my father moved with his wife Irene from Bury in Lancashire to Guernsey after the Second World War, he began to work as a labourer in greenhouses. It was heavy work, especially when steaming the ground with huge iron pans, working through the night to minimise the cost of hiring a steam boiler. On one occasion my father had been shifting ground in huge barrels and had strained muscles in his groin, causing an inguinal hernia.

My father simply ignored the pain, thinking it was just muscle strain, but one night his heart began to pound and he became feverish and began vomiting – the hernia bulge had strangulated.

My parents did not have a telephone in the house yet, so my mother quickly put on a coat and shoes and ran down to the telephone box at Vazon Bay, half a mile away, in the pitch black with just a torch to show her the way. She called an ambulance, praying that it would come quickly and wondering if my father would survive as he reeled in agony back at home.

With a strangulated hernia, a section of bowel becomes trapped and its blood supply is cut off, and this requires emergency surgery within hours to release the trapped tissue and restore its blood supply so it doesn't die.

The ambulance arrived at our home 'Glenside' just as mum got back from the telephone box. My father was taken to hospital and immediately underwent surgery. The doctor told my father when he had come through the surgery that the hernia had ruptured and if he hadn't come to hospital that night, he could have been dead by morning.

I was not yet born, so if it hadn't been for my mother's desperate run down to the telephone box that night, I would not be here to tell this story. I truly believe that God prompted her to get help urgently.

Spared from a Fatal Car Accident

On Friday, 12th September 1975, I had dressed in my flared denim jeans and denim jacket, which was embroidered with flowers, and I had put my wide leather belt on, carved with cowboy symbols, which I had bought at the Greenbelt Music Festival that year. My parents had taken me to the festival, which was held in the grounds of Odell Castle in Bedfordshire. I was just fourteen, but loved Christian rock music and had sat out for hours on a rug on the grass listening to 'Parchment', 'Liberation Suite' and 'After the Fire'. It was the year that I transitioned from a boy to an adolescent and from a shy reserved lad, who would be constantly embarrassed, to an outgoing, creative and determined young teenager with a passion for the guitar.

It was now a Friday evening, and this particular evening a car treasure hunt had been organised for the youth group. I stood on the back step of the church looking across the car park, filled with eager drivers and teams being handed the clues which they would have to find and the items they would have to collect before returning back to the church; the first one back would receive a prize. I had no one to go with and all the cars seemed to be full, until the youth leader shouted to me and said I could go with two boys and a girl in their car. I didn't know them at all and was reluctant to join them, but thought I might as well; otherwise I would miss out on the evening.

I started to walk towards their car, and as I did so, I heard someone I knew shout, "We've got room for one more, Mike. You can come with us."

I waved a 'thank you' to the two boys and the girl who had offered me a lift and jumped into my friend's car, and off we went around the Island finding the clues.

Guernsey is just nine miles by three, and twenty-four square miles in area, so it is easy to drive around it in an hour. We returned and handed in our papers. I can't remember if we won or not, but it had been a great evening and I walked home around 9.30pm, as we lived just fifteen minutes' walk away from the church.

I did hear someone say that they had seen a car accident on the coast road with ambulances and police, but I never gave it a second thought. The following day it was reported on the local news that a car carrying two boys and a girl had been speeding along the Vazon coast road and had hit a curb and spun out of control. One of the boys, aged just seventeen, had died at the scene, and another passenger was critically injured. They had been taking part in a church-organised car treasure hunt! As I heard the report, the colour drained from my face as I realised that I could have been in that car. If it hadn't been for my friend, 25th September 1975 could have been the day that I died or was seriously injured.

I felt so sorry for the young people in the car, and as a result of that fatal accident, time limits or time bonuses on car treasure hunts in the Island were prohibited.

Cayman Isles

Having left school in July 1979 on a Friday after completing my A-levels, I started work at a merchant bank on the Monday. I had worked there in sterling banking and foreign exchange for two years, before I left to join another merchant bank and to train in trust and company administration. I was there three years and then started work at Guinness Mahon Trust Company in 1984. It was here that I began to have an interest in working oversees. The managing director, Mr Eric Pavitt, was a kind and caring man, and I spoke to him about the possibility of working in the Cayman office. He was keen to help me and immediately called the managing director in Cayman and put the wheels in motion for me to go with Bev to live and work in Cayman on a two-year contract. The idea of living and working on a Caribbean island sounded amazing, and we were both looking forward to the experience. Shortly afterwards, Bev said she was expecting. We hadn't really thought about how it would be for her to give birth in Cayman. We did a lot of research, prayed about it, and we both felt uneasy about taking up this position. So I spoke with Mr Pavitt and told him that we had decided not to take up the contract and why. He was very understanding and called the Cayman office to tell them.

Our baby was due to be born in May 1985, but four weeks before his due date, Bev suddenly experienced high blood pressure and had to go for rest in hospital. She was feeling very unwell on the way to the hospital and I had to stop the car along the road so she could get out and be sick.

Neither of us realised at the time how ill she was, and at the hospital they tried everything they could to bring her blood pressure down, but to no avail.

She had pre-eclampsia, which was something I had never heard of, and only afterwards did I realise that she could have died. They carried out an emergency C-section and I was unable to be in the theatre with her, so I sat outside in the corridor and I saw my son, just 5lbs 3ozs, being wheeled out of the theatre in an incubator at 5.30pm on 24th April 1985.

It was a further two hours before my wife was wheeled out and taken to a private room to recover. Then it was three days before Bev was fully *compos mentis* and understood she had had a baby.

Due to what she experienced under the anaesthetic, to this day she is convinced that she died on the operating table and had to be resuscitated.

It was afterwards that we realised how important it was that we had had our baby in Guernsey and not in Cayman, where there wouldn't have been the facilities to cope with such a difficult birth, and we thanked God that we were both convinced that we should not take up that contract.

Malawi

As I have already mentioned, in May 2005 I travelled to Malawi with missionary David Le Page. At that time I was pastoring a small church in Guernsey called Patria Christian Fellowship, and David Le Page was spending much of his time in Africa but was based in Guernsey. He asked if I would like to accompany him on a trip to preach at the National Pastors' Conference, and I was delighted to accept.

I had flown from London to Nairobi and had managed to find him in the middle of a huge crowd in transit at the airport, before we flew together to Lilongwe. It was through David's preaching that Sunday at my home church back in 1969 that I had given my life to Jesus, and so it was such a privilege to be asked by him to preach and teach at the Church of God Malawi National Pastors' Conference in Blantyre.

Born in Guernsey, David had gone to Bible college as a young man, and once ordained, he pastored an Elim church in Alloa near Stirling in Scotland. When a romance began to blossom with a church member called Jean Williamson, Elim Church Headquarters decided to move him to Wales! David continued to write to Jean and she knew that his heart's desire was to be a missionary to Africa. In 1962 he packed two suitcases and sailed to South Africa, where he conducted a crusade meeting for the Full Gospel Church of God, who offered him a church in Lesotho and then one in Rhodesia (now Zimbabwe). Jean sailed to Africa to join him, and they were immediately married there on her arrival. In 1969 David and Jean and their two young children, Sandra and Lloyd, returned to Guernsey on furlough for six months. It was during this time that David preached at the Vazon Mission where, at the age of eight, I gave my life to Jesus.

The family were then given a church to pastor in the newly independent country of Malawi (formerly Nyasaland). Malawi is bordered by Mozambique to the east, south and south-east, by Zambia to the west and by Tanzania to the east and north-east. Lake Malawi dominates the country, accounting for one fifth of its landmass. There are two main cities – Lilongwe in the north and Blantyre (named after the birthplace of David Livingstone) in the south.

The organisation David worked with was the Church of God, a Pentecostal denomination with its base in Cleveland, Tennessee. David planted churches across Malawi and helped build many to his own design (based on the design of the Vazon

67

Elim Church in Guernsey which was built by his father Jim Le Page).

They saw many people come to receive Jesus Christ as their Saviour and Lord during their years in Malawi but it certainly was not without incidents. On one occasion the people from the church at Vazon in Guernsey were called to pray for Jean as she was seriously ill. She was in such a serious condition that she was flown to London for medical help and was admitted to the University College London Hospital after the London School of Hygiene and Tropical Medicine determined that she had contracted cerebral malaria and that her kidneys were failing. She was in intensive care in a coma for eight days with both Tropical Diseases and Renal specialists caring for her. The family were warned that if she would come through alive there was a strong possibility that she would have hearing and visual issues at the very least due to the high quinine doses she was on, and that kidney problems would likely persist. Thank God, she survived this ordeal and was also free from any effects of either the malaria or the treatment.

There were also other incidents where God provided protection for them, and whilst on my trip to Malawi in 2005, David told me three remarkable stories.

The River Crossing

David was travelling one Sunday morning in Betty, a 1968 Land Rover, which had faithfully carried him, his wife Jean and their two children around Malawi for many years. It had been repaired time and time again and had coped with thousands of miles of dirt tracks and pot-holes and off-road driving. This morning he was driving with a local pastor down a familiar road near the Nkhoma Falls, about two hours' drive from

Blantyre, to attend a local church service. It was a steep hill which had a sharp right turn at the bottom and a bridge across the river. The bridge across the river was wooden and had a three to four metre span. There had been heavy rains recently, so the river was running high.

David drove at speed down the hill, and as he turned the corner to drive over the bridge, he realised too late that the bridge was gone, washed away by the torrent. There was no time to brake, no time to swerve, no time even to think; the heavy Land Rover should have plunged into the fast-flowing river – but for God! The Land Rover shot over the three to four metre gap and landed safely on the other side. David said that he felt that the Land Rover had been "lifted and carried" across the gap.

David was shocked, relieved and so grateful to God. As he told this story around the churches wherever he travelled to preach, he gave all the glory to God for saving his life and the life of that local pastor that day. He said that there was no rational explanation for the Land Rover to jump that gap, and he believed that this truly was a miracle of God's protection.

A Black Mamba

David told me that whilst he was preaching in a packed church one Sunday morning, a black mamba snake slithered through the door into the church.

By way of background, the black mamba is a species of highly venomous snake from the elapid family (which includes cobras), and is native to sub-Saharan Africa. The black mamba is considered by many scientists to be one of the most venomous animals in the world, making it one of the most feared snakes on the African continent due to its aggression and potent venom. These can grow up to fourteen feet long and travel as fast as twelve miles per hour. The bite of a black mamba can cause collapse in humans within forty-five minutes and death between seven to fifteen hours. Now, black mambas tend to avoid noise and crowds of people, so it was very unusual to see one enter a church which was full of people.

The people by the doorway were screaming and moving backwards away from the snake as it slithered up the aisle towards David. Without hesitation, he left the lectern and ran towards it shouting, "Out, out, out! In the name of the Jesus, out!" It immediately turned and shot out the church door and disappeared into the grass.

Two Angels?

David told me another remarkable story which concerned Betty. He and Jean were driving in Phalombe, which was close to the Mulanje Mountain, south of Lake Chilwa. They were driving in the dark in torrential rain and there were many crisscrossing paths and tracks; he was completely lost. Betty's headlights were really dim and didn't really show much of the way ahead.

He needed to find the main road, and as he drove around the many muddy tracks, he began to pray for God to guide him and help him find it. Suddenly, in the headlights he saw an African man standing in the rain pointing to the right. He decided to turn right. A little further ahead he saw in the headlights another African man pointing to the left, and as he turned left, he realised he was on the main road out of the town.

Were these two men that God had placed there in the dark and torrential rain to guide him to the safety of the main road, or were they angels? Whatever the explanation, it was certainly a miracle.

We see clearly in the Bible that angels can have the appearance of men. In Genesis 19 two angels visit Lot in Sodom and the men of the city surround the house and demand that Lot hands them over to them. In Genesis 18:2 we read:

> *Abraham looked up and saw three men standing nearby. When he saw them, he hurried from the entrance of his tent to meet them and bowed low to the ground.*

We learn that these men were actually angels who looked like, or took on the appearance of, men.

Hebrews 13:2 tells us:

> *Do not forget to show hospitality to strangers, for by so doing some people have shown hospitality to angels without knowing it.*

It would appear that angels can take on the appearance of human beings and they are here among us to help and protect us.

> *Are not all angels ministering spirits sent to serve those who will inherit salvation?*
>
> *Hebrews 1:14*

> *The angel of the LORD encamps around those who fear him, and he delivers them.*
>
> *Psalm 34:7*

In Matthew 18:10 Jesus says:

> *See that you do not despise one of these little ones.*
> *For I tell you that their angels in heaven always see*
> *the face of my Father in heaven.*

There is an account of John Paton who was a missionary in the New Hebrides islands. One night hostile natives surrounded the mission station, intent on burning out the Patons and killing them. Paton and his wife prayed during that terror-filled night that God would deliver them. When daylight came they were amazed to see their attackers leave. A year later the chief of the tribe was converted to Christ. Remembering what had happened, Paton asked the chief what had kept him from burning down the house and killing them. The chief replied in surprise, "Who were all those men with you there?" Paton knew no men were present – but the chief said he was afraid to attack because he had seen hundreds of big men in shining garments with drawn swords circling the mission station.

I wonder how many times we have been protected and helped by an angel whom we thought was a person…

I believe that I saw an angel on two occasions, maybe the same one. Here are my stories:

A Flat Tyre in France

It was August 2003. Bev and I had decided to have a holiday in France with our eleven-year-old daughter Zara. We had a good friend called Georgina, or 'George' as she was known, and after her husband, our dear friend Andrew, had died in a motorcycle accident, she had decided to move with her young daughter to Côtes-d'Armor in France to run a gîte. We took the ferry from St Peter Port to St Malo and stayed with her for a night, before driving down via Nantes to Ruffec in Charente, where we stayed for a week in a gîte. Then on the following Saturday, we drove from Ruffec to Royon, where we stayed in another gîte for a week in a small town called St Sulpice de Royen. On Friday, 29th August, we packed our cases and loaded them into the car to begin the seven-and-a-half-hour drive back to our friend George in Plouha, to spend one more night in the gîte before returning home on the ferry the following day.

As we turned on to the main road and waited at the road junction to take a left and head for the motorway north, a car stopped across the road from us and a man wearing a beret was frantically pointing at our car. I got out of the car to try and see what was concerning him, and checked our front tyres, but they were fine, then the back left-hand tyre and that was also fine, but the back right-hand tyre was dangerously flat. I looked up to wave a 'thank you' to the man, but the car had disappeared. I couldn't see it anywhere down the road. I then realised that there was no way that he could have seen the back right-hand tyre from where he was!

I am convinced to this day that the man was an angel, and if we had driven for seven-and-a-half hours on the motorway, we could well have had a blowout and a very serious accident.

As it was, I drove to the garage a short distance away and inflated the tyres before continuing on our journey.

A Dangerous Icy Road

We did not often have snow in Guernsey, however, we did have the occasional flurry and sometimes black ice on the roads. It was one of those rare occasions when the snow had been falling all night; because the people in Guernsey were not used to these conditions, they would often walk to work rather than risk having an accident in their cars. The Island is only nine miles by three miles, so for those working in the main town of St Peter Port and living within a couple of miles of the centre, a thirty-minute walk in was not an issue. We lived in St Sampsons in the north of the Island, so it was a fifty-minute walk into the town from our home. I was feeling lazy, so I took the risk and drove the car into the town, and the roads were fairly clear of traffic. I had put a shovel in the boot of the car and a couple of planks of wood in case it snowed some more and I had to dig around the tyres to get the car moving at the end of the business day. I guess I was smiling to myself as I drove passed dozens of people walking on the slippery pavements to town.

Coming home later that day, the temperature had dropped and the roads were very icy. I had almost reached home and had turned into our lane, when the car started to slide to the left and headed towards a granite wall. I tried to brake but that had no effect, so I braced myself for a collision. But it did not happen. I looked to the left of the car where the wall was, and there was a man in a beret standing there with his hands on the car stopping it from sliding into the wall. He motioned with his head for me to keep driving forward, and as I did so, he pushed the car away from the wall and back into the middle of the road, where the tyres gripped once more and I cautiously drove towards my home. As I drove away, I looked in my rear mirror and side mirrors, and he was gone. The wall was at least a hundred feet long, it was high and had no gaps in it. The man in the beret had simply disappeared.

I have no other explanation except that it was the angel, once again saving me from an accident, even though I had actually been foolish to drive in such conditions. How I thank God for his grace!

A Foot That Would Not Move

It was a sunny day, not unusual for Guernsey. I was back working full-time at Deutsche Bank, having spent five years working part-time for my home church in the afternoons and evenings. The department head of the trust division had been promoted and they needed me back to oversee the team. So I had agreed to go full-time for a two-year period until they found someone else to manage the team. I had had a lovely lunch at a restaurant along the sea front with a friend and was now walking back to the office. I had pressed the button on the lights to cross St Julian's Avenue, the widest road in Guernsey, with three lanes of traffic at the bottom of the hill leading to the roundabout and one lane going up. Many of the roads in the Island are only really wide enough for single traffic, but mounting the pavements is allowed and often necessary. I was day-dreaming as I stood there on the pavement waiting for the lights to turn red so I could cross. The green man started to flash and the lights beeped at me, beckoning me to cross. I did not check the traffic, I simply went to lift my right leg and step on to the road. To my annoyance and bewilderment, I could not seem to move my foot. It was as if it was glued to the tarmac or someone was holding it down. I tried again to lift my foot but nothing happened; it seemed like my brain was telling my foot to rise but my foot was either not receiving the command or it stubbornly decided it was not going to move. Just then, I heard the roar of a motor and looked up to see a black transit van shoot through the red lights a metre or so in front of my eyes; I could see the driver talking on his mobile phone.

I stood on the pavement in shock, watching the van speed up to the roundabout and turn left along the sea front. The realisation of how close I had been to death hit me. If I had stepped out on to the crossing, I would have taken the full force of the van and quite possibly been badly injured or killed. I pressed the button once more thinking that the only possible reason for my foot refusing to move was the providence and protection of God. Maybe it was an angel holding down my foot.

The green man started to flash again and the beeping indicated that it was OK to cross. This time I looked to my right and made sure that the traffic had stopped. To walk back to the office, I could pass the police station; having made a note of the name of the catering firm on the van, I went into the reception and was soon sitting with a police officer telling him how close I had come to being run over because a van driver was on his mobile phone. I never heard whether the driver was found or prosecuted, but one thing I know for sure: God saved my life that day, and if he saved my life, it must be for a reason.

One thing that I have learnt through the years is that if someone is healed or a miracle happens, it is always to glorify God. The healing or miracle may benefit you or another person but that's not the primary purpose for God's intervention – it's always about the kingdom.

Canada Shooting

In May 2012, Bev and I, along with our daughter Zara, who was nineteen at the time and had just moved to Scotland to be with us after staying three years with our friends in Guernsey, started a trip around the world. My mum and dad had passed away within four weeks of each other in 2011 and some of our inheritance had come through, so we decided to fly to Sydney, Australia to see our son Yohsan, as we had not seen him for four years, and then to Canada to see our daughter Yolanda who was working in Niagara as a nanny. We decided that as it was a once-in-a-lifetime trip, we would travel club class too!

We timed our trip to Australia for our son's graduation, as he was receiving a degree in contemporary ministry from the Alphacrucis College.

We then flew on to Toronto, via Hawaii, and met Yolanda at Toronto Airport, where we picked up a huge four-by-four and stayed in Canada for a week, driving up into the lakes for a holiday with her.

We decided to stay in Toronto one night before driving to Muskoka, and arrived in the city on Saturday, 2nd June 2012. We parked the truck at the hotel and then visited the CN Tower, went to the top and did the obligatory walk across the glass floor 1,122 feet above the pavement below.

After our visit to the tower, we headed for the Eaton Mall. Bev, Yolanda, Zara and I walked into the entrance of the mall; it was just before 5pm. We looked around a bookshop near the entrance and then the ladies had to go and use the facilities before we headed to the food hall to eat, as we were really hungry.

I stood by a pillar facing the steps going up into the main part of the mall, and I suddenly had a feeling of dread and impending trouble. It was not the first time that I had had this gut-wrenching feeling before something bad happened.

When the ladies returned, I said to them that I thought we should go back to the hotel right away and we could come back to the mall later.

I was amazed that they all agreed. After all, we were in a shopping centre!

We left the mall at 5.15pm and walked to the Metropolitan Hotel, just a few hundred yards away, and went up to our rooms to rest up. A while later we turned on the news and saw that at 6.20pm there had been a shooting in the food hall of the Eaton Mall; one person was dead and six people were injured. The mall was in lockdown and police were moving in.

We realised that we would have been eating in the food hall when the shooting had taken place and the Holy Spirit had warned me about it, saving us from potential injury or even death.

We ordered room service rather than venture out again that evening!

A Whirlwind

My father had been a grower, working in the horticulture industry since he arrived in the Island after the Second World War. He had purchased the house which my grandfather had built in six weeks back in 1925, and where my mother and her siblings had grown up. The house was made from wood, had block gable ends and an asbestos roof. It had weathered many storms.

To the back of the house there was a large plot of land on which we grew hundreds of pots of freesias and a 120-foot by 30-foot greenhouse. To the side of the house were two further greenhouses, each 190-foot by 30-foot.

In the early seventies my father decided to sell the two large greenhouses to a neighbour but kept the 120-foot greenhouse behind the house, even though it was only a couple of feet from the first of the neighbours' greenhouses. The details here are important as you will discover.

I was at school one day and my mother was working in the back kitchen at home, when she heard what sounded like a heavy lorry roaring up the road past the house and then the sound of hundreds of panes of glass smashing. She ran outside to see that the two greenhouses that my father used to own were completely demolished. It would appear that a whirlwind had roared up the road past the wooden house, turned at the corner of the house and demolished the two greenhouses completely, but had not damaged the house or the greenhouse behind us.

If the whirlwind had hit the house, it would have been demolished too. It is my conclusion that God protected our home and my mother who was there at the time.

It was not uncommon for whirlwinds to roll in off the sea, and our home was just a few hundred yards from the beach. I once saw a house overlooking an area of grassy common with a row of tiles completely stripped off its roof.

However, there was another miracle of protection at my home church a year or two later. We had come to the end of the morning service and were singing the last hymn. It was around 12.30pm. Whilst we were singing, we heard over the music what sounded like heavy hail on the roof. A few minutes later we walked out into the car park, which was covered in shards of broken glass. A whirlwind had come in off the sea and hit the greenhouses behind the church, ripped off many dozens of panes of glass and dropped them on the church roof and the cars in the carpark. If the service had finished five minutes earlier and everyone had been in the carpark, talking and going to their cars, there could have been some serious injuries. Once again, God was protecting us.

7

Miracles of Provision

The Rent Money

My mother and father, before they purchased 'Glenside', rented the house and greenhouses from my grandfather. My dad gave my grandfather cash each month to settle the rent payment. One day he went to get the envelope with the rent money in, which he had left on a unit by the back door, and could not find it. He frantically looked around the floor and around the other units, but it was nowhere to be found. He tried to think where it could be but could not imagine how it could have moved from the unit. That night he woke up and remembered that he had placed a bundle of newspapers on the unit before taking them and burning them on a bonfire down the garden. He realised that the envelope must have got caught up in the papers and put on the fire. He began to pray that somehow God would have prevented the fire from burning the envelope, even though that would have to be a miracle. At first light he got out of bed, dressed and made his way down the garden where there was a pile of ashes. He took a stick and began to search in the ashes, still believing that God would answer his prayer.

Suddenly the stick revealed an envelope which was charred but not burnt through. He reached down into the ashes, took the envelope and opened it. There were the bank notes, with just a few singes, but intact and still legal tender. My parents lived hand to mouth and could not have paid the rent if God had not provided for them in this miraculous way. My father used to give this testimony and would show the people the charred envelope.

Ralph Winter Smith

Bev and I had been praying about pastors who suffered from burnout. Our friend Pastor Bob Miles had told me that no one who graduated from Bible college with him was still in ministry, due to stress, and this really bothered us. We had an inkling at the time that we would end up in some form of ministry, so we decided to create an upper room in our home where pastors and their wives could come and stay for a few days, a week or longer. We saw many in ministry arrive looking totally worn out, but when they left, mainly due to the glorious Guernsey sunshine, they were rested and refreshed and ready to get back to their ministry. We also used it to provide accommodation for visiting speakers who would come across to the Island to preach at the Vazon Elim Church or minister at a united churches seminar or conference, and one of the ministers who came to minister and stayed with us was Pastor Ralph Winter Smith. Whilst visiting us on 6th October 2002, he recounted two remarkable stories of God's provision for them. Here are his stories in his own words.

The Blue Sierra

What happened was, I was driving an old, beat-up car and needed a new one. I had no money so started to ask God for a replacement car. Cars for me are just a tool of the trade, so I needed one and it had to be reliable.

My approach in cases like this is to spend time seeking God in patches until I get an answer. So, for example, in my prayer time I might spend some time each day (or a few times a week) within that prayer time just asking for and listening about a car (or whatever) until I am sure.

In this case, as I prayed over a shortish period of time (maybe a few days), I started to think about a blue Sierra, then a diesel blue Sierra, then one with non-electric windows, and a clear request formed which I considered had been given to me by God, so that's what I asked for. I just believed for the car out of this prayer / waiting time.

A short time later, I received a phone call and was offered as a gift a blue Sierra, diesel, non-electric windows, 80,000 miles on the clock but only three years old. This was the answer. I kept that car for ten years and it served me well. It never broke down, although towards the end of my ownership it did overheat sometimes.

I should add, I had not told anyone about my prayers before the gift of the car.

The Piano

My eldest daughter wanted to learn to play the piano. She was about six at the time. I was keen to help, and to make it work she needed a piano. I had no money so I sat down with my two daughters and wife and we just prayed a simple prayer, asking God to give us a piano. Then I said we should do something to show we believed God had heard our prayer and would provide a piano. We all agreed.

To make it practical, I said we should move things around in the living room to make room for the piano when it arrived. I said, "Where shall we put it?" We agreed we would put it along the wall where at that time stood a small dresser with a fish tank on top. So we moved the fish tank and dresser to the other side of the room.

When we had done that, we held hands and danced around for a bit, thanking and praising God for the piano. Yep, we really did!

About six weeks later, one evening my daughter asked me when the piano would arrive. I said, "Soon, darling." I just believed that.

A couple of days later, a lady we knew rang us out of the blue and asked if we knew anyone who would like a piano as her auntie had died and left her to clear the house, including disposing of the piano her auntie had.

I thanked her and said we would like it. I had not told anyone about our prayer.

I had to hire a man and van to move the piano. He dealt in pianos so was equipped with a trolley, a van and two strong men. When he arrived, before he took the piano out of the van, he asked me if I wanted to sell it to him for £250. That was in 1980 so you can see the piano was not junk. Of course I declined, thinking no way was I selling what God had given us. It came with a proper stool too and we had not asked God for that!

The man asked where the piano was to go and I showed him the spot. He told me it was too big and would not fit the designated spot. Immediately I knew it would fit since God would not provide a piano too big for the spot we had in faith prepared.

The piano fitted, and the door which broke in two the wall along which the piano was to sit cleared the end of the piano by about 1½ inches. Perfect! Of course.

If I was explaining these two incidents, in the first case I would say God gave a word which became the basis for my faith, but I did believe as I heard. In the second case I would say we just believed God would answer our prayer without him giving any word of knowledge as we prayed.

God is good and it has blessed me to recall these events.

As well as these stories, Bev and I have also experienced remarkable miracles of provision.

Bradford Minibus

Whilst I was serving as the pastor of the Patria Christian Fellowship, I decided to attend a worship conference in Bradford at the Abundant Life Church, and I took my worship leader and his wife with me. The three of us flew from Guernsey to Manchester and then took a train to Bradford, where we stayed at the Holiday Inn Express overnight to attend the conference the next morning.

The hotel was part of a complex which included a cinema and ten pin bowling centre, so crowds of people were milling around outside the hotel. We were waiting at the top of some steps for someone to pick up my worship leader and his wife, and felt nervous at the number of youths circling around us, so we quickly moved to another area to wait. The next morning we met up again for breakfast and it was starting to rain outside. I said to my companions that we needed to pray for someone with three spare seats in a minibus to pick us up and take us to the church, especially as it was quite a walk there and we were nervous about our safety.

We left the hotel and began to walk down the street. I said to my worship leader, "Where's our minibus?" Just as I said it, a minibus drew up alongside us and a man in the front passenger seat wound down the window and asked, "Do you know the way to Abundant Life Church?" I replied that I did and we were heading there ourselves. He told us to jump in as there were three spare seats!

I directed them along Shipley Airedale Road, up Otley Road and into Wapping Road. This was one of the most specific answers I have received to a specific prayer. I learnt that day to be specific when asking God for things.

Protection and Provision Whilst Working at the Bank

Both Bev and I had been working in banking and finance in the Island of Guernsey all our lives, apart from when Bev took some time out to raise our children.

One evening in 1999, as I was driving along the coast road by Cobo Bay on the way to a prayer meeting, I heard a voice in my head say clearly, "You can't serve me with dirty hands." It was a bit of a shock! I went to the prayer meeting and then returned home, and as I was praying about this, I felt that the Holy Spirit was telling me that I needed to change my working arrangements. As a senior manager in the bank, I had to act as Director and Trustee to a number of client cases, some of whom, although not evading tax, were probably setting up offshore structures for unethical reasons, and I had no choice but to be part of the governance of those fiduciary vehicles. I had no idea how to extract myself from these companies without quitting my job. Shortly afterwards I had a strong feeling that I should ask my managing director if I could work part-time for the bank, as I had a desire to work part-time for my local church. No one in such a senior position had ever been granted a part time position, so I popped upstairs to see the CEO of the bank. I told him what was on my mind, and without hesitation he said that he was happy to arrange a position for me; in fact, there was a new department starting up to risk manage the business and I could work a twenty-five-hour week, mornings only, in that new department. This meant that I could not continue to hold trustee or director positions for these client structures, which of course freed me from being involved in anything that could 'dirty my hands'. Not only that, I was now in a position to recommend the termination or transfer of any client structure which I believed to be a higher risk to the bank! God is simply amazing!

This happened very quickly, and on 7th September that year, I started work in risk management. My salary had been cut drastically, which meant that Bev had to go back to work full-time to pay the mortgage and I was demoted in this new role. What I did not realise when I changed position was that I would also lose my company car (a rather nice, red Mazda MX3 coupe) and my pension, as part-time staff could not have these benefits. I simply trusted God and believed that he would provide for us. In the meantime I was going door-to-door with Pastor Paul Gower around the Vazon Bay area of the Island visiting around 1,500 homes over a period of a few weeks. When we finished, we started again at the beginning, so there was consistency in our visits to homes. I was still expected to carry a company phone and to be the main contact for a high net worth client from South America, and I remember walking down the road one sunny afternoon towards the church on a call from the client's lawyer, discussing the setting up of another trust for him and thinking, if only he knew where I was and what I had been doing, going door to door telling people about Jesus!

In January 2000, I received a letter from the bank telling me that by law all part-time staff had to receive the same benefits as full-time staff and that my pension payments would therefore be resumed with immediate effect. It was a huge relief (but I did not get my nice, red Mazda back!)

Lose a Job / Gain a Job

I was asked in 2005 by the then CEO if I would consider heading up the trust team again full-time for two years, on the understanding that I would need to get away sharp every day for church-related work. I agreed, although it put immense strain on me as I was studying through distance learning for my theology degree, working full-time in a high-pressure job, pastoring a church and looking after my family. Then in 2006 a new CEO was appointed and he proceeded to dismiss many of the senior managers.

I had just returned from a wonderful trip around South America with my wife, which we had taken to celebrate our Silver Wedding Anniversary. On the second day back in the office, I received an email from my manager stating that the arrangements I had (to be able to leave on time in order to run the church) were not working any more and that I should consider my position. I knew that this was coming from the CEO, because before I left on holiday he had asked me to be the head of both the Guernsey and Geneva offices, spending two weeks every month in Geneva. There was no way that I could do this and pastor the church, and I did not want to be away from my wife and family every month. He had been angry at my refusal to do this, so it came as no surprise that he had planned to oust me from my position on my return.

Having suddenly had my job taken away and still a large mortgage to pay and three children at home, it was a challenging moment, but God answered my prayer for help and within a few minutes of being told I was out of a job, I walked down the corridor and bumped into the COO in charge of the back office. He could see from my face that I was not my usual, happy, smiling self and asked what the problem was. When I told him, I could see that he was angry that this had happened to me. He immediately said, "I can't let you go – you have a wealth of experience. I will create a job for you, if you'll come and work for me." So the following week I moved from front office into back office and became the project manager. I was promoted to Senior Associate Director and received an increase in salary.

The story has an amusing twist to it and with this, and on several other occasions, I have realised that God has a sense of humour. The following year I was given the task of establishing a trust company in Mumbai, and having no previous experience of establishing a trust company from scratch, I spent a week thinking it through and putting a ten-step project plan in place. Then I was told by the COO that the CEO had lost his position and that he had been demoted and, in fact, he would now be working for me. That put me in an interesting position! I could treat him however I wanted to treat him!

In fact, it was obvious what to do; I welcomed him into the team and, by the grace of God, never acted in any way towards him except kindly and graciously.

Protection from Terrorist Attack

I knew that the former CEO had previously established a trust company, so I asked if he would review the project plan and suggest any amendments, additional steps or considerations required. After review, he said that there was nothing he could add, which was incredibly reassuring. Having already travelled to Mumbai myself, I asked him to attend the next meeting, and we planned for him to be in Mumbai on Wednesday, 26th November 2008, staying at The Oberoi hotel.

You will no doubt remember that on Wednesday, 26th November 2008, ten members of Lashkar-e-Taiba, an extremist Islamist terrorist organisation based in Pakistan, carried out twelve coordinated shooting and bombing attacks, lasting four days, across Mumbai, and 174 people died, including nine attackers, and more than three hundred were wounded. They were held up for four days in The Oberoi, where my colleague would have been staying if it had not been for our decision to postpone that visit.

I called him the following morning, as he was in our Swiss office, and said how pleased I was that his trip had been cancelled and that he was not at the hotel as originally planned. He said to me, "I think someone was watching over me."

He was Jewish and would have been a prime target for the extremists.

Provision of Accommodation for our Daughter

On Monday, 15th September that same year, I received a phone call from the Elim regional leader for the Metropolitan region saying that the pastoral care pastor was retiring from ministry at Chelmsford Elim (now renamed Life Church Chelmsford). He said that Mike Sherwood, the senior pastor, whom I knew, had been looking through the Ministers Directory praying about who could come and replace him, and he saw my name and felt the Holy Spirit tell him that I was the minister to approach about the position.

I had just finished painting every room in the house, as I knew that we were going to have to sell it. I had no idea that it would be because we would be asked to leave the Island where we had lived for forty-seven years and a house we had lived in for twenty-two years.

We went for the interview and took our two daughters, Yolanda and Zara, aged twenty-one and sixteen respectively, and the following day we were shopping in Oxford Street, looking for a hat for Bev because we also had the small matter of our son's wedding coming up in the December; at the time, he was in Australia. While in the hat shop, I received a phone call from Mike saying that the board had decided to offer me the position.

Initially we were all jumping around in the shop excited, but then, when we went to have a coffee, we all realised that everything was about to change and nothing would be the same again. We would be selling the home the children had all grown up in and leaving an island that we loved. Everyone just cried. I have no idea what the people in the coffee shop thought was happening!

We then had the difficult decision to make concerning Zara, who had just started studying for her A-Levels. We went to visit a couple of schools in Chelmsford but neither could transfer her subjects, so it became obvious that we would have to leave our sixteen-year-old daughter behind on the Island.

We prayed that someone would offer to look after her for two years whilst she stayed and studied. It was impractical for her to stay with either of her grandparents and we could not think of anyone she could stay with. So we prayed that God would provide her with a home and a family. Almost immediately we received a call from our friends Nigel and Sue, offering to look after her in their home. The decision to leave her behind was heart-breaking, but it certainly was the right decision as she continued her education at the grammar school and gained four A-levels, three at A* and one A. Staying in Guernsey was as hard for her as it was for us as her parents. Whenever there was a parents' evening or a letter for parents, her teacher would say to her, "Ah yes, you don't have parents here, do you?" I have no idea how she coped with being left alone at the age of sixteen but somehow God got us through it, and aged nineteen she moved across to Scotland to live with us.

Provision for a Car Loan

In 2008, having accepted the position as Pastoral Care Pastor at the Elim Chelmsford, Bev and I started to work our notice at the banks where we were employed. I wrote out my resignation letter and went into my boss's office to hand it in. He passed it back to me and said to hold on to it until he asked me for it. I thought that this was rather odd but did so anyway. I told him the date I would be leaving in March 2009.

We had a car loan of £6,300 from the bank Bev worked for; this had to be repaid before she left, and we had no savings. All our funds were tied up in the value of our house which we were struggling to sell. We did not worry about the car loan but prayed and trusted God in it. The time of our departure was drawing near when suddenly my boss called me into his office. I sat down and he handed me an envelope. I asked him what it was and he said that it was the staff bonuses day; even though I would not have been entitled to a bonus if I had handed in my notice, he was not going to let me go without giving me a bonus, because of the hard work I had put in that previous year. I was stunned, as I did not expect this to happen. When I opened the envelope, I could have wept, as the cheque was for £6,300. My boss then said to me, "You can hand in your notice to me now."

Yahweh Yireh – God is my provider.

House Sales and Purchases

Bev and I had moved from Guernsey to Chelmsford in March 2009. Our house took some time to sell and God provided a home for us in a cottage in a wood in Little Baddow near Danbury. A lovely lady called June owned a huge house there with a cottage attached, because she and her husband had ten children and her husband had built the house big enough to accommodate them all. By the time we met her, she was alone in the house, but welcomed missionaries on furlough to stay and others in ministry like us. I had checked my mortgage paperwork and found a mortgage holiday clause that said we could, on one occasion only, ask the lender for up to six months of no mortgage repayments. This was great because our bank salaries had stopped and my pastor's salary was a third of what we had been earning, so we could not have afforded to keep paying the mortgage. The mortgage holiday ended in September 2009. We were at the Elim Conference in Prestatyn in June that year, and I received a phone call from the estate agent saying that someone had put an offer on our house in Guernsey. I felt that it was too low below the asking price so turned it down. They called back with an increased offer and once again I felt it was too low. They came back with a third and final offer which we accepted, and we exchanged contracts at the end of July and repaid our mortgage with just a few weeks to spare!

We found a house in Langford near Maldon which we liked, even though it needed a lot of work, and purchased it, moving out of June's little cottage in late August 2009.

We saw amazing things happen whilst we were there in Chelmsford, and to this day consider these to be the best two years of our ministry.

One day I was in the church office, when reception called me to say that a man had walked in asking to see a pastor. I went downstairs thinking that he was probably after money. It was common for people to come into the church reception asking for money, and we knew whatever complex, elaborate stories they came out with, it was sadly just to feed their habits of drugs or alcohol.

However, this man, who was in his mid-thirties, sat down in our church lounge area and said that he was a backslidden Christian and as he was walking past the church, the Holy Spirit told him to go into the church, find a pastor and repent. So I had the tremendous joy, there and then, of leading him back to Christ.

On another occasion, I was talking to people after one of the two services we ran on a Sunday morning, when a man, probably in his mid-fifties, said to me that he had been walking past the church the previous afternoon on his way home to hang himself but had heard a voice telling him to go to that church the next morning, and that was why he was there. I had the joy of praying with him there and then for salvation.

I organised a number of men's events, one of which was the visit of the Tough Talk team, made up of ex-cons and doormen who had found Christ and now travelled around churches pushing weights and telling their stories. One man who came that night was Adam. He was probably in his late thirties, and built like a brick house. He was the man who lifted the heaviest weights that night, and he came on an Alpha course and gave his life to Christ. When we left Chelmsford, he kept in contact via Facebook and, shockingly, one day I saw a message from his mother on his Facebook page saying that he had died. I knew that his decision for Christ was genuine and messaged his mother to reassure her. Then I thought, "What if Adam hadn't come that night? What if he hadn't heard the gospel and responded?"

Then came a bit of an issue for us as a couple. We had moved from Guernsey in 2009 to work with the senior pastor, who then retired in 2011. The church board asked me to succeed him and become the senior pastor. However, due to some communication confusion, another minister was invited to take up the role. We were devastated and confused, having felt certain that we were meant to step into that role to develop and grow the church.

We also believed that God wanted the church to rent and then purchase the electricity buildings next door which would have provided the church with a huge complex accommodating a nursery, a youth area, a conference room, offices, a potential Christian-run gym and coffee shop, and a dance floor for teaching performing arts. The project was making progress and we were in negotiation with the Electricity Company, but then they had a change of CEO and the opportunity was lost.

It seemed like everything we had hoped for and planned for had come crashing down around us, and we did not know what to do.

We prayed and asked God to tell us whether we should continue ministering in Chelmsford or whether he had other plans for us. In fact, we were attending the Hillsong Europe conference at the O2 at the time and asked specifically that God would tell us at the conference whether we should stay or go. Bishop T. D. Jakes was preaching on the last night and his subject was Abraham and Isaac. As he was speaking, he stopped and said, "There are some of you here tonight and God is taking you to a place, and where you are is not it. When you return from this conference, there will be a shift in your circumstances." Bev and I looked at each other and we knew that God was going to move us on.

Two weeks later I received a phone call from Regional Leader Kevin Peat, who introduced himself and said, "I don't know you and you don't know me, but I'm here with John Glass, the General Superintendent, and we wonder whether you would move to Kilsyth?"

I did not know where Kilsyth was, but I already knew this was the shift in our circumstances.

On Sunday, 13th November 2012, we told the church that we were leaving, and there was a sense of shock and upset. There was a long queue of people who wanted to see us after the service to say how much they would miss us. It was a very emotionally challenging time for both of us as we loved the people so much and still do.

As we were preparing to leave, I asked God for one final confirmation that this was his plan for us and I put out a fleece like Gideon.[4]

I said to God, "Please confirm this is your will by selling our house in three days."

The house next door to us had just sold after six months on the market, and the house across the road had been on the market for eighteen months and had not sold yet. We put our house on the market on the Friday, someone came to see it on the Saturday and they put an offer in on the Monday, and it was sold.

In fact, it sold whilst we were up in Scotland looking at a house to rent which belonged to the church treasurer. We were having lunch in Kilsyth when the offer came through on our house, and we accepted; then, half an hour later, the treasurer met us at his house and said that he was actually looking to sell it, and we made an offer and it was accepted. We also bought all his furniture, even his pictures and vases and lawnmower etc. He called us as we were leaving Essex and asked if we would like him to make our bed up! It was the easiest move ever.

---

[4] See Judges 6:36-40.

End Note

Many people have asked me if I have ever doubted my faith, and I can honestly say that I have not. Hopefully, on reading this book, you will realise why.

If you are not yet a follower of Jesus Christ, I would implore you to take a step of faith, as I did, and see how amazing life can be with Christ. If you have not experienced the baptism in the Holy Spirit, then maybe you will be encouraged to know that ordinary people filled with the Holy Spirit can achieve extraordinary things through his power and authority.

We only live once, so do not waste time but live your life to the full, in and through Jesus Christ, who loves you more than you will ever fully understand.

Similar Books from the Publisher

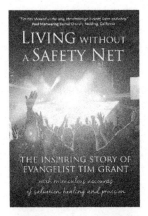

Living without a Safety Net
Tim Grant
ISBN 978-1-911086-35-2

Packed with remarkable accounts of healings, miracles and salvation, this book tells how healing evangelist Tim Grant encountered Jesus in his early life and how he learned to walk by faith and bring Christ's love to countless lives.

Grace and Glory
Stephen & Julie Jonathan
ISBN 978-1-78815-748-3

The inspiring story of the impact one small church had on their local community, told by pastors Stephen and Julie Jonathan.

Available from your local Christian bookshop
or from the publishers:

onwardsandupwards.org/shop